DIGITAL STORYTELLING

Capturing Lives, Creating Community

Joe Lambert

DIGITAL STORYTELLING

Capturing Lives, Creating Community

Digital Diner Press
Berkeley, California, USA

Digital Diner Press
1803 Martin Luther King, Jr. Way
Berkeley, CA 94709
510 548 2065 phone
510 548 1345 fax
www.storycenter.org

ISBN: 0-9726440-0-8

Book Design by Oakleaf Designs, Patrick and Eileen Milligan
Cover Design by Joe Lambert, Emily Paulos and Jos Sances
Graphics by Jos Sances, Alliance Graphics
Printed by Central Plains Book Manufacturing

First Edition

All proceeds to benefit the Scholarship Fund of the Center for Digital Storytelling, a project of Life On The Water, Inc., a California non-profit corporation, 94-2660844.

Printed in the United States of America

Acknowledgments

On behalf of my collaborators at the Center for Digital Storytelling, I would like to graciously thank a number of people for their contributions to the development of the *Digital Storytelling—Capturing Lives, Creating Community*.

To start with, we would like to thank the thousands of students who have shared their lives and stories with us and inspire our work. In particular, we want to thank Barbara French, Frank Gonzalez, Ernesto Ayala, Daniel Weinshenker, Monte Hallis, and Ann Jaeger for allowing us to share their stories. We have the greatest job in the world, and in every workshop we expand our circle of friends.

The first Digital Storytelling Workshop was at the American Film Institute in Los Angeles, and we want to thank Nick DiMartino, Harry Mott and Harry Marks who have been part of this bus from the very beginning.

We must recognize that this book itself has seeds in two projects. In 1996 we were given support by Apple Computer, led by our friends Ralph Rogers and Kelli Richards, to create the original *Digital Storytelling Cookbook*. Then in 1998, the Institute for the Future, with particular support from our friends Kathi Vian and Bob Johansen, gave us support for *Digital Storytelling—The Creative Application of Digital Technology to the Ancient Art of Storytelling*.

We have a number of associates, including Amy Hill, Caleb Paull, and Thenmozhi Soundararajan who are interviewed in the book, as well as Denise Atchley, Barbara Aragon, Kevin Gordon, and Leslie Rule, who act as our principal producers, respondents and friends, without which our work would not be possible. In addition members of Board of Directors, and the particular support of our friends Abbe Don and Mitchell Yawitz in the last year breathed confidence into our efforts.

Our work has received consistent and generous support from Adobe Systems. Special thanks to Russell Brown at Adobe, for his long-term and continuing encouragement.

Over the years Digital Storytelling has evolved beyond our studios and our workshops with practices in numerous contexts. We look back to recognize the importance of our collaboration with the Digital Clubhouse Network and our friends Warren Hegg, Mary Ellen Locke and many others in informing the expansion of our approach. We also are more recently indebted to the efforts of our international colleagues. We thank Sayoko Ogata, Satoko Michishita, Eiko Kamiyama, Michio Komatsuzaki and Akio Kikucki at Proseed in Tokyo for help-ing us to look much closer at our work. We also want to recognize the particular feedback and support we have received in our work with BBC-Wales through our colleague Daniel Meadows. In addition we recognize our collaborations with Geska Helena Andersson, Philip Petersen, Jonas Michenek, and Julia Granath in Sweden and Denmark, our work in Australia with Helen Simondson at the Australian Center of the Moving Image, our collaboration in Canada, with Ana Serrano and other friends MediaLink Habitat at the Canadian Film Centre, and finally Jan Bieringa at Evision, in Wellington, New Zealand.

The work on this book was made possible principally as a collaboration with Emily Paulos, the administrative director at CDS. Her support and guidance was critical to the last ditch effort to finally get this book out. We also want to shout out a big thanks to Eileen and Patrick Milligan at Oakleaf Designs, for their efforts in the book design and editing, and to Jos Sances, who helped us with the cover design and graphic elements.

Finally, as a book of ideas, inspired by the Digital Storytelling Workshop, this is really about my collaboration with Nina Mullen and Dana Atchley.

Nina Mullen has taken this journey with me to all parts of the world. Our col-laboration informs every aspect of this book, and in that sense, she shares authorship through me. In the face of the ups and downs of our work, her clar-ity and commitment is astounding, and I am grateful to be her life and work partner. I missed quite a few nights at home with Massimo, our son, and our yet-to-named, yet-to-be born daughter, so a big hug to them.

Dana Atchley and I took the original trip on *Next Exit* sixteen years ago. His exit in 2000 was unbearably heartbreaking. His spirit sits over my left shoulder, guiding me through this work. He would have enjoyed this book. So Dana, thanks again, buddy.

For Dana Atchley
Artist, Friend, Digital Storyteller
Your final exit was beyond reason.
Your vision will live on.
See you on the flipside.

Contents

DIGITAL STORYTELLING

Capturing Lives, Creating Community

Introduction

When possible, elucidate the plainly apparent, as the most obscure wisdom.

—*Joey Eddy Buddha*
Zen Master of the Obvious

Writing down the story of one's work is a generally healthy exercise. Believing that someone else in this great wide world of ours will find it useful or insightful is, well, common sense. Or perhaps not.

In any event, having traveled ten years down this path of work, it seemed appropriate to attempt this publication. We have every reason to believe more and more people are interested in using multimedia tools to look at the events of their lives. They probably would appreciate some ideas about how to approach this work. And there are now scores of people that have begun to define themselves as facilitators of digital storytelling, and they too, can probably save themselves a bit of time by listening to those of us who have spent several years helping others in this process.

Having said that, the main role of an introduction is to suggest what kind of glasses you should put on to consume the writing that follows. Since we have not met, you and I, we should chat a moment about your expectations.

I want you to know that I view myself first and foremost as a practitioner, someone who enjoys working with people and making things happen. An old colleague of mine, artist Terry Allen, had a saying that talking about Art is like French kissing on the telephone. I feel that way about most efforts to eff the ineffable. Talking about what it is you do and why you do it, if you are driven by deep passions as most of us are, is not even a close proximate of the actual experience of doing it.

You will find a couple of contextual essays about the history and vision of our work in this volume; six chapters that talk about how you might make a digital story and use it for your personal or professional needs, and six chapters that discuss how digital storytelling has been taught and applied. This suggests that it is both a text book and a teacher's guide. In essence, this book is a long conversation about an idea, the idea of digital storytelling in all its current permutations.

So I have opinions. Many. And sharing those opinions helps me test my own sanity and perspective. Our work has not been thoroughly researched, and the opinions are based on large piles of empiricism, which may mean that they are slightly incorrect, or plain stupid. I respect you, my dear reader, to let me know your own opinion. My email is jello@well.com.

The Re-Storification of Our Culture

Personal storytelling, in the forms of recitation and creative writing, had a renaissance in the 1990s. Educators, business people, creative designers, and community activists all found themselves drawn to idea, as author and storytelling consultant Richard Stone has described it, of the "restorification" of our culture. Stone sees modern culture, and many of us would agree, as having clear-cut away our use of story as cultural glue. In traditional cultures, the intermingling of personal stories, communal stories, myths, legends and folktales not only entertained us, but created a powerful empathetic bond between ourselves and our communities. Like the environmental process where we are now attempting to recover the forests that were swept away by industrial logging methods, we are facing a painful but critical process to find ways to integrate story back into our lives.

Stone and others have pointed to electronic media and accompanying lifestyles as the principal antagonist in this tragedy. Television, and the family and personal habits that occur when the television acts as the hearth of our home, undoubtedly complicates our ability to claim our own stories and honor the legacies of communal memory that are rooted in our biological ancestries.

While we fully agree that broadcast television media creates enormous social problems, we do not identify the media itself as the main problem. As we moved from oral cultures to a world where the written word had primacy in communication, we lost a range of social practices that had enormous value in our communities. As we dropped our books and flocked to movie theaters, more quickly scanned our newspapers and magazines and turned on our radios—as we stopped reading entirely and watch TV an average of 7 hours a day (as is found in the US)—there were losses, one after the other.

But none of the forms went away entirely. Many cultures, particularly those who have only recently had a place at the banquet table of modern middle class lifestyle, never lost their sense of story, and the role of story in their culture. They have much to teach us in our re-storifying process. We still talk a great deal about our lives, and about the books, films and television we consume. People find ways to gather. Many families have reclaimed the dining hours as storied social ritual, and make camping trips communal story exchanges as often as they can. Some of us also write. We have composed letters to each other, penned poems to our sweethearts, and pounded out essays, pamphlets and books. Story has been part of all of these exchanges, and we can build deeper senses of listening, understanding and composition from this foundation.

When I look back at the last year, and the unapologetically reflective and sincere storytelling that occurred in the U.S. in response to September 11, I can also feel a validation of this larger process of bringing our story exchanges back to the center of our culture.

At the Center for Digital Storytelling, we believe we can use media, ironically, to overcome the more troublesome residual effects of our consumer media culture. The digital storytelling community has described the Internet and new media explosion as a release to a century of pent up frustration at being involved in a one way discourse, electronic media speaks at us but we could not talk back. We want to talk back, not on the terms of the governors of media empires, but on our own terms. We want the full diversity of expressions to be available, even if we ignore most of them, most of the time. The fact there is a web page on the art of spaghetti sculpture, with flash narratives and a how-to video, somehow comforts us. That could be our obsession, our signifying experience, open for an exchange with a community of like-minded spaghetti sculptors around the world. Even if we never visit, we rejoice to know we could.

With video and audio production achieving a technical complexity and affordability that is only slightly more involved than learning the QWERTY typewriter, we will want to use those forms. We need not duplicate a use of media that services the entertainment industry, filling screens for hours to rationalize advertising time. We can decide to make short films that invite responses in spoken word, text, and other short films.

Those of us committed to story as a healing process, can emphasize the listening, the exchange, the solemnity of life passage, that re-invest storytelling with the meaning it deserves. In that world, the green forest's tens of millions of stories, will find ways to enrich all of our lives.

My Story

The last couple of years have had plenty of larger dramas that put most of us in the position of a shared story of terrorism, war, and economic crisis. These are weighty stories, that put our personal losses and struggles in perspective.

In my own case, 2000 and 2001 represented a series of losses, my brother Maury, my close friend and partner, Dana, and finally my mother, Latane.

When death entered my life at this close proximity, and with a relentless sequence, the story that defined me changed. I would like to share with you my story.

I essentially grew up in a nuclear family of four. While there were three brothers, my oldest brother, David, was off to college before the end of my first year of life, and his role in my life, was that of a loving, but relatively distant, mentor. My mother, my father, my slightly older brother, Maury, and I shared most of the significant moments of my childhood—first steps, first words, starting school, riding bikes, fights and injuries, teenage tests and tragedies.

My father died when I was seventeen, a few days after I finished high school. I left my native Texas within a year and a few months, and relocated to California, in essence, for good. Back in Austin, my mom and brother represented home.

With them gone, with the family house sold, there is a rupture in my memory. I can no longer touch and be in the place of return called the family home.

My brother's death was the most tragic. At 45, he had just completed a seven-year sojourn in training himself for the twenty first century. He went from being a security guard and bus driver to an engineer responsible for operating a half-billion dollar machinery that produces the chips running the computers that dominate our lives.

After his last class at the local college in May of 2000, he joined my 83-year old mom for a trip to Vancouver Island. They toured, and walked beaches with old friends, ate and prepared meals together, and I am sure, laughed and quarreled with each other in equal doses of intensity.

Maury came back angry. Ostensibly at my mom, for an offense in all other contexts would be trivial. His anger tipped the scale of his life. A day after his return, he died.

Thirty-five job offers awaited him.

When a mirror image of yourself—a brother that looked into your face at your birth with the wonder of a two year old, who blazed trails and fought battles for you, who knew you at your worst and most frightened, who applauded your challenges and celebrated your successes—is gone, with no warning, you fall long, and hard, and forever.

In truth, I knew my brother had already died many deaths. His was the life of the tragic hero with fatal flaws of too much love, too much passion, too much courage, and much too much anger at his own image of his imperfection. His self-loathing drove him inside the walls of his ego, where the world could not touch him. Neither friends nor loved ones could save him.

In as much as we share the same DNA, the same embattled youth, the same resolute bullheadedness about wrong and right and meaning, I now see the shadow of my own death.

Sobering.

My brother's middle name was Maverick. Though dissolved a bit in meaning by Hollywood and corporate brandings, my connection to the name is loud and clear. I come from a family of political mavericks in the South. I grew to share their sense of the quixotic adventure for social justice and empowerment, and to make choices in my own life that would leave me running free from the herd. Like my brother, I remain angry enough to be unforgiving of deceit, of hypocrisy, of injustice. Like him, my frustrations lead me too often to journey to the well of loneliness.

But I collect stories. And share my own. And I know that with this process, this maverick can find a return, can make himself at home, and find family, wherever I go. I am alive, and in my brother's memory, and the memory of my family and friend Dana, carry on the job before me.

I look forward to your stories.

Joe Lambert
October 2002

1 A Road Traveled

Evolution of the Digital Storytelling Practice

Every process has a genesis story—an arbitrary point in time to call...the beginning.

When did digital storytelling begin? When I speak for a larger notion of digital storytelling, I always feel compelled to go back to the 1960's, and the spirit of democratization and humanism that forms both the politic and the practice of this work.

When I speak for myself, my version of the story has two parts, my work in politics and theater in San Francisco, and the story of when I met Dana, Dana Atchley, that is, and I try and recall his walking into the construction site that was our theater in the Fall of 1986.

And finally, I think of the moment it really made sense to anyone else, the first workshop that was held at the American Film Institute in 1993.

Wherever the beginning really occurred, the important idea is that something new coalesced around this work, and that our trying to name and understand this process is still very much evolving.

So climb up into the cab of our 18-wheel time machine and let's drive back on the road taken.

Story, Folk Songs, and the American Tradition of Celebrating Lives Lived

When I was a kid, my parents liked to host parties at our little house in Dallas, Texas. Over the years, lots of people showed up at our house, the local politicos and labor movement people, friends and neighbors, and often the sojourning activists and artists that found our home a small oasis of liberal friendliness in the desert of 1950's Texas conservatism.

Of course my favorite people were the folksingers.

The bardic tradition was resurrected in the name of social urgency in 20th century America. Joe Hill and the Wobblies found that by re-writing commentary to the tune of Salvation Army hymnals they could capture the lives and issues of working people as social protest. Blues, always a reportage of life and living, found broader audience and captured new meaning in the context of a century of post-slavery African-American struggle that came center stage in post-WWII American politics. Woody Guthrie lifted the Western ballad, traditional tunes for European folk culture adapted to the frontier experience, and told the stories of dustbowl desperation and New Deal optimism.

The lesion in memory of the McCarthy era could not completely erase the insurgence of the democratic impulse in American music, and with one section of the rock and roll culture surfacing in the 1950's, the folk music scene provided a vital line of continuity between these voices of the centuries first half, and the explosive cultural renovation that marked it's seventh decade.

Digital storytelling is rooted fundamentally in the notion of democratized culture that was the hallmark of the folk music, re-claimed folk culture, and cultural activists traditions of the 1960's.

As Greil Marcus wrote about the feelings inspired by the American folk music culture, *"No one is just like anybody else. No one, in fact, is even who he or she was ever supposed to be. No one was supposed to step out from their fellows and stand alone to say their piece, to thrill those who stand and listen with the notion that they, too, might have a voice ..." Granta, 2002*

Inherently sympathetic to human experience, the voices of these storytellers looked for ways to capture their own and others sense of the extraordinary in the ordinary comings and goings of life. Where a mainstream culture provided glamorized and idealized lives of the movie star-perfect people living in dramatic and exotic situations, the populist artist in the folk traditions sought not just to portray, but to empower. This new folk culture spread as the leading artists worked to help to find a guitar for each person in countless living rooms, music halls, and outdoor gatherings, teach them eight chords, a set of licks, and song forms that could be grasped, and set them off to record their own experience.

All the artistic disciplines became caught up in the democratization process of the era. In literature, new voices of women and people of color were found in the greatly expanded notion of author and authority. In theater and dance, companies were formed to transform oral histories of common people into productions of broad impact and scope, often involving the respondents in the production as actors, writers and designers. In the visual arts, community muralism, youth arts, media interventions and countless other riffs on the "Art for the People" idea came into being.

The legacy of this era informs educational, therapeutic, social service, professional and civic processes in countless ways. The methods of capturing stories, reflecting on and analyzing how stories are told, encouraging thoughtful insights about one's own experience, all changed in the face of social movement cultures that shaped the public discourse for 15 years. On a level of profound understanding, people who had the professional task of encouraging the learning, growth, and stability of other people, realized that the sense of significance that resulted when a person "found their voice, and made their story heard" was fundamental to our healthy living.

We can live better as celebrated contributors, we can easily die from our perceived lack of significance to others, to our community, to our society.

The Texan Gets Baptized in the Revolution

When I speak of my own road, I found myself in San Francisco in 1976, bouncing around the debates of post-sixties revolutionary politics. One sector of that politics was consumed with the debates about race and social change. In the practice of criticism/self-criticism that was a currency of this kind of politics, I found large sectors of my Texas white boy identity being sheered away as part of transformative re-generation, toward creating the "New" Joe Lambert, intricately aware of my own racism, sexism, subjectivity and socioeconomically predetermined consciousness. In retrospect, while there was something naïve and a bit weird about this process of political correctness and multicultural immersion, there was also something liberating.

In his book, *The Politics of Authenticity: Liberalism, Christianity, and the New Left in America*, author Doug Rossinow, discusses how other activists emerging from the white Southern, and specifically white Texan, backgrounds in the sixties tended their "conversions" to political rebelliousness as a transcendental moment. It wasn't that most of us had spiritual education (for myself, almost none) it was just that the languages of spiritual renewal were so prevalent in all aspects of the cultures around us, that using this language seemed to provide legitimacy to our crossing over to an outsider stance to the dominant culture. In deciding to link our perspective with the victims of the project of American settlement and empire, having shared some of the abundance created by that project, we felt fear and rupture. We were leaving home, both psychically, and for many, like me, physically. But we were also being baptized into a new world of possibility, and the potential for a fluid, expansive identity that connected us to the motion of history.

San Francisco's cultural environment made it easy to cross over. I learned Chinese and hung out with Asian American activists in Chinatown and the Nihonmachi (Japantown). I danced to salsa, soul, and disco in the Latino Mission district. I went out to organize tenants in the housing projects of the African-American Hunter's Point. My references of identity, the stories that I connected with, were becoming less about people that looked like me and shared my background, and more about people that I thought were heroically struggling to re-make a world beyond the legacies of oppression, racial mistrust, and class hierarchies. They just happened to be Black, Brown, Red and Yellow, for the most part, and as such, I became a bit more identified with the syntax, language and story of those cultures in America.

Life and Life On The Water

From this perspective I entered the cultural field as a professional theater person, having trained in dramatic theory, literature and writing, as well as the politics and sociology of art, at UC Berkeley. From 1983-86, I worked for, and then directed, the People's Theater Coalition (PTC), a non-profit organization that ran a theater, worked as an advocacy and networking service for almost 20 other local theaters, and for a couple of years, ran a training academy. The wave of popular theater work in the seventies had crested and broken on the beaches of the reality of the Reagan 80's, and the PTC was itself in pieces as I took over.

I spent a couple of years holding on, and then re-organized my planning and development work to start a new operation in the Fall of 1986. With luck, I found three willing collaborators, Bill Talen, Ellen Sebastian and Leonard Pitt, successful experimentalists in various theatrical styles, to join me. We formed Life On The Water (LOH2O) in 1986, and opened our first season with Spalding Gray's *Swimming to Cambodia*.

Life On The Water had many things going for it. We emerged at a time when experimentation in theater, having belonged appropriately in marginal avant-garde, was somehow becoming mainstream. The eighties began US culture's colonization of the "Culture of Cool." The trend to trend-hop in search of traces of authenticity meant those on the margins suddenly had a place at the table of the national dialogue. This process was institutionalized in the social democratic countries of the developed world where the Avant Garde became official culture in 1980s, but in the States it was a hit-or-miss affair. Actors like Whoopi Goldberg, Willem Defoe, John Malkovich, Anna Deveare Smith and John Leguizamo, coming from various experimental theater communities, could slip through the cracks and become Hollywood talent, but a whole host of other, extraordinarily talented performers could barely make ends meet. Careers of musical artists like Tracy Chapman, who was "Talkin' about Revolution," and scores of artists in the Rap Music boom, found mainstream acceptance right smack in the middle of the conservative Reagan years. Multiculturalism and the formal languages of inclusion permeated the Art world, even as federal grants were being cut, and the relative incomes of the rich and poor, of White and People of Color, separated into the current yawning gulf.

Ironies Abound.

Our theater featured an eclectic mix of experimental and community-based artists, one week we would have the latest of the East Village hipsters, the next a local Chicano Theater company. But perhaps we were best known as a home to Solo Performance, a quintessentially eighties art-form. Contemporary solo theater had it's roots in the performance art experiments in the 1960's visual arts communities, the community theater artists' connecting with and claiming the folk tradition of "storytelling," and the collapse of the non-profit arts economy in the early eighties. Solo was cheap to produce. Half of the productions at LOH2O were solo works.

Life On The Water, along with our sister theater Climate, ran a national festival of solo performance, Solo Mio, from 1990 to 1995. It was in this context that I met and began my collaboration with Dana Atchley.

The Colorado Spaceman Exits in San Francisco

Dana Atchley wandered into Life On The Water just before we opened in 1986. Our theater was being re-modeled, based on a design by architect Minoru Takeyama, on a budget of 10 cents, and a timeline of the day before yesterday. As such, a few days before the season opened the place still looked like a construction site. Dana stepped over a few 2 x 4's and introduced himself. At 45, he was approximately the same age as our season opener, Spalding Gray. And like Spalding, he had a mix of New England WASP carriage, with a twist of road wisdom and perspective. In retrospect, I think they both shared the baby boom pioneer role. Most of what middle-class white people in the U.S. experienced and think of the sixties first happened in the Northeast United States in the late fifties, before it leaped to West Coast. They were there.

Dana had a show, or and idea of one, and wanted to know if we would be interested in collaborating. I agreed to go over and visit and have him give me a tour of his life's work. The show was called *Next Exit*, and it was exactly that, a guided tour of Dana's life. His idea was captured inside a large three ring binder, he said, and opening the binder there were four pages of storyboards, that described some of the stories, and the layout of his stage. I looked up at him, and back at the binder, and then back at him again. "Okay ... uh, so what can we do?" I asked.

Dana explained that for the last 20 years he had been traveling around the country collecting roadside Americana, and stories about offbeat Americans, as a sort of artistic practice. In the seventies, the project was a touring show called *Roadshow* which had him singing, telling stories, and projecting slides of these oddities, touring from college to college to art school to community center. In the eighties he had taken on the role of commercial video producer, working for Showtime, Evening Magazine, and French Television, producing short "Video Postcards" in the context of licensing his content to commercial sources. Dana missed the stage, and wanted to build this show to get back into the arts after his seven-year hiatus.

I explained the situation of fundraising, programming, and management of the project, as I did to numerous artists wanting to be produced by our theater. As I left, I am sure I thought, "He's too ambitious, and he needs to develop more of project before we can search for support. I wish him luck." I did not really think it would go anywhere.

Well, Dana didn't fade away. He stayed close to our theater, assisting with some video documentation of one of our performances, joining us at special events and openings. The next time we met, the three ring binder had 50 pages, and he had three or four new pieces to show me that he had produced for the show. I agreed to write a few grants for the project, and somewhat as I expected, they were not funded. In the Spring of 1990, Dana said he would produce the work on his own, in his Mission District Studio. I said I thought that would make sense, a workshopping process, and I agreed to help with the show, and to link it to our first Solo Mio Festival.

In September of 1990, Dana did a four-week run at his studio. At this point, the binder was full, and Dana had about 40 episodes organized into an hour plus of a performance. The central metaphor was the campfire, Dana entered the stage and sat down next to a video monitor that he would "light" and it would play a tape loop of a roaring campfire. Behind him was a large projected backdrop, usually a Drive-in movie theater outline inside of which the various video segments would screen. Dana would then both narrate and interact with the video segments as they advanced.

As this started, Dana was forced to rely an operator/stage hand assisting him in starting and stopping the video deck. In his first performances, this naturally led to a mechanical performance as he slowed down or speeded up his narration to remain in sync with the video segments in parts of the performance. This was less than satisfactory.

But even in these early performances, Dana's design choices and approach to the subjects of *Next Exit* encouraged many people who watched the performance to say, yes, I have a story like this. His subject matter concerned five decades of his life. He had stories of his youth and activities such as camp, elementary school crushes, learning to drive, and his father's obsession with ham radio. He had stories of his college days and coming of age as a young artist, his mentors, his travels, and his marriage and divorce. He had stories of the beginning of his days as a traveling performer/experimental artist in the seventies, and the many colorful characters he met upon the road, and the loneliness he felt in spending time away from his children. And finally he had stories of his days as a professional video producer covering hundreds of thousands of miles shooting an odd assortment of American attractions.

Dana was an Ivy League trained graphic artist, and had over a decade of work in video, but his design approach was for the most part transparent. He chose very approachable icons (the road and myth of the American highway, the campfire, the big painted skys of the West, Americana, the family album, home movies) and interpreted those icons through video segments that while superbly produced, rarely called attention to their refinement. His own performance style was direct and informal, conversational, which also tended to diminish the distance between him as performer and his audience.

Next Exit survived a couple of runs in his studio in 1990, but in 1991, with my and other's encouragement, he went back and re-wrote the piece to make the performance more coherent, and to examine and re-tool the technologies he used for executing the evening. The 1991 performance run had him intertwining the themes of the evening effectively, and ending the performance on a more focused, and transcendent note. He also traded the video decks for Laser Discs that could be controlled by a MIDI software on a computer, giving him increased flexibility in performance.

By 1992, the show began to travel around the Technology and Arts network of exhibitions, trade shows, and special events around California. As part of this process, Dana was introduced to the possibility of bringing his videos onto the computer through the great improvements in Apple Computer's Quicktime technology. He met and began a long collaboration with Patrick Milligan, an interactive authoring design professional. Patrick adapted Dana's set backdrop design that had been accomplished with slide and video projectors, and created a computer-based interface with Macromedia's Director tool.

Computer Art had generally been associated with conceptually "cool" and experimental expression, demonstrating what the "computer" could create as much as the point of view of the artist-creator. In this context, *Next Exit* was a sharp contrast. Populist, transparent, and emotionally direct, Dana's performance spoke directly to a large section of the new media audience that still liked to hear a good story, well told.

An Exit Called Hollywood—
1993 at the American Film Institute

One of the great ironies of Dana Atchley's personal story was that in 1980 he was approached by a producer with Lorimar Productions (the people that brought you Dallas) with a made-for-TV offer on his life as a traveling artist collecting Americana. Dana signed an initial agreement for a relatively small amount of money. When the movie deal fell through, for various reasons, the fine print stipulated that the character he portrayed in Roadshow, the Ace of

Space, was no longer his. He had sold his identity, and a small part of his soul, to the devil, and as he told it, he spent his 40th birthday in 1981 in the town of Nothing, Arizona. When you've seen Nothing, you've seen everything.

Thus it probably confounded him a bit when he received a call in the Fall of 1992 from the American Film Institute in Los Angeles to be a featured performer at their upcoming National Video Festival. He was also asked to lead a workshop in their brand new Digital Media computer lab, having people make short personal video stories, inspired by Dana's example.

The backdrop for this event was what could only be called the Digital Tsunami of 1992 in California. The San Francisco Bay Area happened to host that place called Silicon Valley. As such, the engineers had been letting artists play with their toys for three decades. When the potential of desktop computing reached the frontier of multimedia, still and moving image, text and sound, there was a thunderous explosion of activity. Just before the Dot-com boom, was the Interactive Media mini-boom. Money appeared out of nowhere, artists jumped ship from photography, film/video, graphic design, radio and television to try and position themselves in the "second gold rush" they perceived was occurring before their eyes.

In San Francisco, Dana invited me to an exhibition of work at a local professional meeting, the International Interactive Communications Society, and the feeling in the room was electric. The hundred person capacity room was overflowing with people. I invited the group to hold their next meeting at my 200 seat theater, but 400 people showed up four weeks later. I caught the bug, led by collaborators in the performing arts like Mark Petrakis and Randall Packer, and saw the need for the performing arts community to be in dialogue with this sector.

When Dana, Patrick and I arrived in Los Angeles, in February of 1993, we felt confident that we would make a good impression. Dana's performance had improved, the technology was increasingly stable, and the audience was going to be folks that could easily spread the word about this show. Of course, the idea of spending a weekend learning digital video editing intrigued me particularly, because while I had worked closely with Dana in the video production, and had seen the toolsets demonstrated, I hadn't yet put stories together myself.

In fact, the show nearly had a disastrous beginning. Dana had made some adjustments, and the computer and the projector seemed uninterested in working together. With some last minute work by Patrick, and with me laughing to one side, *Next Exit* was performed. It was a resounding success. In the audience was Dana's future wife and collaborator Denise Aungst, and so impressed was she, that she left making up her mind to marry him.

The workshop had similar effect. The ten or so participants fell into their projects with a demanding intensity. The time flew by, from a Friday night introduction, all day Saturday and Sunday, and then it was time to leave. I made a small piece about my parents wedding in Texas. And while I returned to the Bay Area, the final piece of magic was at the showing of the pieces at a Tuesday night salon hosted by the well-known broadcast designer and digital guru Harry Marks.

One of the participants, Monte Hallis, a production designer in LA, had produced a story about her relationship with a young mother, Tanya, who was carrying on her own battle with AIDS, while trying to organize support for other parents facing terminal illness. As it happened, Monte arrived late to the screening. She set an empty chair before the screen, and reported that Tanya had died just a few hours before. Then this powerful and direct story was premiered. As Dana later reported, there wasn't a dry eye in the house.

Inspirations and Transformations

Dana, Patrick and I returned two more times to Los Angeles in 1993 to lead workshops at the AFI. Each time I felt something in the process that inexplicably moved me. I had experienced drama therapy, group art exchanges, and creative writing courses that were emotionally powerful. But in this process, of turning story into the medium of film (in a couple of days), defied my attempts at characterization. It was "like" many things, but it was also unlike anything I had ever seen before. The sense of transformation of the material, and of accomplishment, went well beyond the familiar forms of creative activity I could reference. And even as the tools themselves frustrated me, I knew that this activity had a special power that could be shaped into a formal creative practice.

I came to understand that the mix of digital photography and non-linear editing are a tremendous play space for people. They can experiment and realize transformations of these familiar objects, the photos, the movies, the artifacts, in a way that enlivens their relationship to the objects. Because this creative play is grounded in important stories the workshop participants want to tell, it can become a transcendent experience.

Those of us who work with story know that in conversational storytelling, around tables and public gatherings, stories lead to stories lead to stories. We can watch the patterns unfold as each story transforms the conversations, the meaning, the exchange, into deeper and more intimate communication. There is so much invisible power in this simple activity that people walk away from some gatherings feeling transformed, but having little or no sense of the process that brought them there.

A critical component of our success in that first year was the inspiration provided by stories that are shown leading into the workshop experience. In 1993, this was created by the design examples in Dana's show. But immediately, stories like Monte Hallis' Tanya, became the examples as they reflected the achievements of the two– and three–day process. Our catalogue of examples became hundreds, and then thousands; we can now show stories on innumerable subjects and contexts if called for by the occasion.

As a result of the AFI experience, numerous events unfolded within a year.

- We had closed down the theater operations of Life On The Water, reducing the organization from 19 people to three.
- I moved Life On The Water to the studio adjacent Dana Atchley's loft in the Mission.
- Dana and I organized what became a long running series of informal salons, Joe's Digital Diner, which brought together leaders in the new media design field.
- Life On The Water took out a $50,000 loan, purchased six workstations and all the audiovisual requirements to offer the digital storytelling classes.
- We produced a six-week Thursday night run of *Next Exit* that was followed by six weeks of digital storytelling workshops in the Spring of 1994.
- We hired a staff member to work on this project, my wife, Nina Mullen.
- Life On The Water began doing business as the San Francisco Digital Media Center and produced a calendar of classes using six different software programs, by a wide array of teachers, including the first html authoring class for the San Francisco community.

Change happened. And the rest was history.

2 Meaning and the Memory Box

Looking back from 2020

We have a seven-year-old son, Massimo. By the year 2020, he will be 25 years old. If all goes as planned, he will be early in his professional work life. At about the same time, again if things go as planned, Nina and I will be looking to retire.

We try to imagine this time.

> *A typical day at the house. Joe sits on the deck with his little Memory Box, Nina is busy gardening.*
>
> *"Nina, could you help me with this thing here?"*
>
> *"Joe, I'm busy trying to get my bulbs in the ground. Can't it wait?"*
>
> *"Just a second, honey. I just want you to look at this."*
>
> *"Oh all right. Are you still trying to make that HC?"*
>
> *"Nina, it's just a little project for the digital storytelling banquet next week, I promised I would get it done by Friday and e-mail it to the staff. Look here, I have this footage back in '02 when Massi was getting his first computer for school. I wanted to show how difficult it was to run those horrid PCs.   But I can't quite figure out how to make the holographic cinema capture that Wintel machine melting right in the old piece of video."*
>
> *"So why don't you call your son and ask him? He's the one who gave you the software."*
>
> *"Good idea. See, you helped, now you can go on back to your bulbs. Thanks, sweetie."*
>
> *"Joe, you never change."*

She exits. He speaks to the box in front of him.

"Get me Massimo, you pile of crap."

A moment's pause. A voice comes over the machine.

"Hello, Noorooz Masonry Design. Massimo speaking."

"Hey, Massi, got a second?"

"Yeah, Dad, what is it this time?"

"Just doing another little story, trying to morph in a little meltdown in an old piece of video, and it ain't working right."

"Why don't you just do it as a character animation? It's so much easier as a cartoon."

"I know—but I like those old special effects, like those stupid movies when I was younger."

"Listen, Dad, I have a presentation in half an hour with a client who expects me to dazzle him, and I want it to be magic. He wants our company to mason an entire facade of a war hero's museum in Novorossiysk and I'm trying to get the dialect down for my presentation. The translation software in my box keeps slipping into Azerbaijani and that could be a disaster. And the rasterizer on my VR modeling deck is barely operational. I may have to improvise the whole thing. So could I call you back?"

"Nouveau riche Russians don't know a damn thing about stonemasonry, son. You can fake it."

"Dad!"

"Okay. Okay. I'll check back. Your mom expects you to come back from Teheran for dinner this weekend, don't forget."

"I'll be there. Bye, Dad."

Again to the machine:

"Just you and me, babe. We're just going to have to figure it out, even if you are a sorry piece of crap. I should probably trade you in for a better model ...

The machine responds. Voice of Lauren Bacall.

"Threats aren't good for your blood pressure, honey, which is 160 over 120 by the way. If you need some help, maybe you should whistle. You know how to whistle don't you? Just put your lips together and blow."

"Damn box, just open the file."

Joe whistles.

Few things are certain about this distance into the future. The world is changing too rapidly for us to know how the myriad technology options in lifestyle support, in workplace design, in civic participation will affect the youthful worker or the retiring professional. But one near certainty, in my mind, is the existence of a machine—perhaps it best be called an appliance —that will be capable of sustaining an exhaustive record of our day-to-day experience: the Memory Box.

Our vision of the Memory Box is an amalgam of the family album, educational portfolio, home video library, scrapbook, record of work-related documents and media, telephone, television, scanner, audio/visual digitizer, training and application tool in every conceivable media type and metaphor of creative expression all wrapped into one. It might even have an attitude. The Memory Box will hook into to an array of wearable and disposable input devices that will allow one to record anything at any time at resolutions far above our current television standards. And of course it will be attached to the Internet, where it will be supplemented by a library of resources of infinite dimension.

For us old folks, the Memory Box will be the home of our family and professional archives. In retirement, we may choose to create multimedia memoirs illustrated with this collection of images and videos, make gifts for friends and family that relate our feelings for them, share our interests in hobbies, or travel experiences with like-minded people. We might even develop political presentations to organize our neighbors to complain about the size of our Social Security checks. It will be how we extend all of the historic forms of interpersonal communication from the face-to-face conversation, the letter, the telephone and electronic mail. We'll grab media files to illustrate our stories as easily as we gesticulate with our hands. Whether or not people will want to listen to us will, of course, depend on how well we learn to tell a story.

For the 20-somethings of the 2020s, this appliance will provide more than hindsight. Whether he is a stonemason or an astrophysicist, Massimo will live in a world where personal media creative expertise will be tantamount to economic survival. His Memory Box will be a tool that can capture and store any experience he deems significant. Massimo will use his Memory Box to draw from any part of his historical educational/life experience portfolio, and the device will assist him in defining the meaning of those experiences and creating stories. During any professional conversation, in presentation to live audiences, or in narrow or broadband mediated representations, he will have the ability to call up a wealth of references as animations, graphics, video, audio, or text.

To reach a level of economic or social security, he will have to combine the production skills of a media creative with the flexibility and shrewdness of the improvisational performer. In other words, he will have to become an excellent digital storyteller.

Digital Literacy

Telling stories about the future is an appropriate way to approach the issues of an inspirational tome. But we are not talking about tomorrow. The Memory Box is the current multimedia personal computer. Thousands of communication-enhancing applications for business and pleasure are being developed each year for the computer. Millions of stories are being constructed in the digital domain every day. How many of us, if we died tomorrow, would be leaving the largest residue of our very existence on the planet etched as digital data on one or another hard drive?

The Memory Box exists, but we are far from becoming elegantly skilled storytellers in these new media. We need a sustained effort of digital literacy to maximize the potential of the current technologies, and to create an informed consumer who can help to shape the technologies of tomorrow. Our experience has demonstrated that project-based learning within the context of personal story greatly accelerates the learning process of multimedia technologies. Anything that can make the process of enhancing communications skills enjoyable and meaningful, as well as efficient, is worth your time.

Conversational Media

This is not a book about developing a screenplay for the digital feature film or authoring the hypertext novel. While these processes are related, what we have in mind is a Memory Box filled with lots of little stories. Put together, they might represent a larger narrative, but they are really meant as singular expressions, available for numerous presentation contexts, from a conversation across a laptop to a 2,000-seat auditorium. We approach the storytelling part of our work as an extension of the kind of everyday storytelling that occurs around the dinner table, the bar, or the campfire.

Creating media within this conversational context also changes the way we think about media in general. We believe it is critical to sustain the human-to-human, face-to-face communication as the central means of our exchange, while media assists and amplifies our ideas in a complementary context. Much of what we help people create would not easily stand alone as broadcast media, but, in the context of conversation, it can be extraordinarily powerful.

Thinking about conversational media shapes the way we will organize the media assets in our Memory Box. The digital images, video, music, texts, and voice will find themselves labeled according to stories and story types. These will reflect our important personal and professional relationships, moral or ethical values, critical intellectual realizations, and most valuable life experiences.

Finally, conversational media suggests that presentation of the material becomes increasingly organic, interactive, and spontaneous. Even as we are deepening our facility with creating media, we will be developing new presentational skills that emphasize improvisation.

Improvisational Identities

The idea of digital storytelling has also resonated with many people because it speaks to an undeniable need to constantly explain our identities to each other. Identity is changing. It used to be that being German or Peruvian meant something definitive about our tastes, religion, and appearance. Our worlds were small enough that geographic or ethnic descriptors were some guarantee of expectation in sorting out appropriate ways to interact with each other. The only real way to know about someone is through story, and not one consistent story, but a number of little stories that can adjust to countless different contexts. As we improvise our ways through our multiple identities, any tool that extends our ability to communicate information about ourselves to others becomes invaluable. The digital stories that will inhabit our Memory Boxes will undoubtedly assist in this larger project of allowing us to coexist in a world of fluid identity.

Looking Backward

When I was 15, my father gave me a copy of a book by Edward Bellamy called *Looking Backward*. Written in the 1890s, it was a Rip Van Winkle sort of story looking 100 years into a future filled with the utopian promise of technological society. It foretold, among other things, the fax machine and something like the Internet.

My father believed in progress. Here, at the beginning of the 21st century, amid new forms of terror and counter-terrorist security measures, with the technology boom of the nineties quickly fading into the rear view mirror, some of the ideas of technological progress seem more than a little foolish.

My father also understood irony. You couldn't work in the labor movement in the American South and not have a full dose of ironic detachment. His message when he handed me that book was not that utopia was possible, but that we have a moral duty to imagine it. And perhaps more than that, we have a responsibility to pass that imagination from generation to generation.

The paradox of using the cutting-edge technology of digital media to encourage, in essence, a return to the ancient values of oral culture would make Dad smile.

Looking backward from 2020 to the Memory Box of today, we have a challenge to change a culture, to adapt, to make meaning out of the efforts of our lives. Whether the promise of the Memory Box and digital storytelling becomes fact or remains a speculation is not that relevant. We need to work toward its potential.

Interlude One

The Legacy of Tanya

I never had a lot of friends, not really…The truth is that I didn't even know what one was… Growing up I was shy and confused friendship with popularity.

Last year I met Tanya and we became the kind of friends that most friends are, acquaintances. She knew she had AIDS and would die soon, but facing death gave her more strength to live.

She had no place to leave her girls and wanted to find them a good home.

Tanya also wanted to start an organization to help parents like herself die in peace knowing their children would love and cared for. She also needed a real friend.

Tanya got a lot of attention the minute she told her story, as if the world had been waiting for her. I stood by and watched in amazement

A few months later she couldn't do much on her own and for all her efforts she felt she had only accomplished one thing…she found a real friend, and it was me…I couldn't let her dreams die with her.

The other night, Tanya told me to lay my head down next to hers. She wanted to tell me a secret… "Monte Fay, don't forget, all we've got is where we're going"….

I couldn't believe she knew my middle name.

Tanya
—Monte Hallis

2003 marks the tenth anniversary of the first Digital Storytelling workshop in early February of 1993. At nearly every workshop I have taught, I have told the story of joining Dana and Patrick Milligan on the ride down to Los Angeles to participate in the workshop. Dana's show had gone well, and we gathered in a classroom on Friday night to meet the students. We went around the room of eight participants, and it seemed promising.

I remember my first impression of Monte Hallis. She was my prototype of the Los Angeles woman; blond, professional, relaxed and self-assertive. At a place like the American Film Institute (AFI), which to an old Texas boy like me seemed like a fairly fancy place, I expected to meet folks like her. Dana was sitting at a desk, sitting on one leg folded back, checking in with folks. Monte described the story of Tanya Shaw, a mother with AIDS, that had inspired a number of people to take up the cause of people like Tanya. Monte wanted to do a story on Tanya as a general profile on her inspiring work. When Monte finished her description of her story idea, I remember Dana saying, "But what does the story have to do with you?" I cannot remember her answer, but I do remember when she came back the next morning, her story had changed. And she had a fire about finishing it.

I spoke with Monte in 1998, and she told me that she stayed up all Saturday night to finish the work. The workshop went well on Sunday, with lots of great first stories. I returned to San Francisco, but Patrick and Dana stayed down for the showing on Tuesday, at Harry Marks' Salon at the AFI. As they described it, the other students arrived, and movies were put on one after another. But no Monte.

She finally came in, and before her movie was shown, she put an empty chair before the large monitor. "I'm sorry I am late. But Tanya died." The movie was shown. Everyone was touched by the moment.

I would suppose, at this time, that not many stories of the thousands we have assisted being made have meant as much to the maker as this meant to Monte. There have been many memorial pieces. I have made several memorial stories myself. But there was something clear, something precise, in the making of this tribute that continues to inspire.

Of the many dedications that we could offer for our work, one would certainly be to Tanya Shaw. By her example of sharing her story to organize others, even in the face of death, we are all taught a valuable lesson about dignity.

3 Stories in Our Lives

A story can be as short as explaining why you bought your first car or house or as long as War and Peace. Your own desires in life, the kinds of struggles you have faced, and, most importantly, the number and depth of realizations you have taken from your experience all shape your natural abilities as an effective storyteller. Translating those realizations into stories in the form of essays, memoirs, autobiographies, short stories, novels, plays, screenplays, or multimedia scripts, is mainly about time. You need time to put the raw material before you, time to learn procedures and approaches for crafting the story, and time to listen to the feedback and improve upon your efforts.

For some, conceiving an idea for a story is an easy process; for others it is the beginning of a crisis. The issue of how we get from our conversational use of story to crafting a work that stands on its own falls more into the category of a general creative process. Why and how do we remember stories? What affects our ability to retain stories? How do we develop our own sense of voice and story? And what kinds of stories from our personal and work lives are likely to work as multimedia stories?

That Reminds Me of a Story

Cultural anthropologist Gregory Bateson was asked in the 1950s if he believed that computer artificial intelligence was possible. He responded that he did not know, but that he believed when you would ask a computer a yes-or-no question and it responded with "that reminds me of a story," you would be close.

Our understanding of how story is at the core of human activity has been a subject of fascination for academics and experts in the computer age. Educational and artificial intelligence theorist Roger Schank has been arguing in the last decade that the road to understanding human intelligence, and therefore to constructing artificial intelligence, is built on story. In Schank's 1992 book, *Tell Me a Story*, he suggests that the cyclical process of developing increasingly complex levels of stories that we apply in increasingly sophisticated ways to specific situations is one way to map the human cognitive development process. Stories are the large and small instruments of meaning, of explanation, that we store in our memories. We cannot live without them.

So why is it that when many of us are asked to construct a story as a formal presentation to illustrate a point, we go blank? We informally tell stories all the time, but the conscious construction of story calls up mental blocks. Here are three possible reasons.

Overloaded Memory Bank

From the standpoint of cognitive theory, the problem is about being overwhelmed by stories that we cannot process. Our minds construct gists of memory immediately after an experience or the hearing of a story, and unless we have a dramatic experience, or have a particular reason to constantly recite the story of the experience, it slowly diminishes in our memory. Retrieval of a given story for application at the point that we are analyzing something or making a judgment naturally becomes more difficult the farther away we are in time from that originating story.

In oral culture, we humans learned to store the stories as epigrams, little tales that had a meaningful proverb at the end. The constant repetition of epigrammatic tales gave us a stock supply of references to put to appropriate use, like the hundreds of cowboy sayings I grew up with in Texas, to apply to a wide range of situations. In our current culture, many of us have not developed an epigrammatic learning equivalent to these processes.

At the same time, we are bombarded with millions of indigestible, literally unmemorable, story fragments every time we pick up a phone, bump into a friend, watch TV, listen to the radio, read a book or a newspaper, or browse the Web. We cannot process these into epigrams, recite and retain them, and so they become a jumble of fragments that actually inhibit our ability to construct a coherent story.

Only people who develop effective filtering, indexing, and repackaging tools in their minds can manage to successfully and consistently articulate meaning that reconstructs as a coherent story. We think of the skilled professionals in any given field as having developed this process for their specialty. They can tell appropriate stories—the memory of cases for a trial lawyer, for example—based on having systematized a portion of their memories. But most skilled professionals have difficulty crossing over into using examples outside their field, from their personal life or nonprofessional experience. Those who do, we often describe as storytellers.

This is one of the arguments for the lifelong Memory Box as a retrieval/filtering/construction system to assist us in this process. Images, videos, sounds, and other representations of events from our life can help us to reconstruct more complete memories and therefore expand the repertoire of story that we can put to use.

The Editor

Having worked in arts education settings, we are experienced with people telling us that they have no story to tell. Along with language arts educators and psychologists, we are aware that as humans most of us carry around a little voice, the editor, that tells us that what we have to say is not entertaining or substantial enough to be heard. That editor is a composite figure of everyone in our lives who diminished our sense of creative ability, from family members, to teachers, to employers, to the society as a whole. We live in a culture where expert story making is a highly valued and rewarded craft.

Once we fall behind in developing our natural storytelling abilities to their fullest extent, it takes a much longer commitment and concentration to reclaim those abilities. As adults, time spent in these creative endeavors is generally considered frivolous and marginal by our society, and so few pursue it. Those of us who have assisted people in trying to reclaim their voice know that it requires a tremendous sensitivity to successfully bring people to a point where they trust that the stories they do tell are vital, emotionally powerful, and unique. Were it not that we as human beings have a deep intuitive sense of the power of story, it's a wonder that we have a popular storytelling tradition at all.

The Good Consumer Habit

Our awareness of the residual impact of mass media has grown tremendously over the past 30 years. Media literacy experts have thoroughly documented that the prolonged exposure to mass media over time disintegrates our critical intelligence. The process is, in part, the effect of the over-stimulation we already mentioned. Yet, beyond the fact that we are immersed in too much TV and other media, it is the style in which these media, particularly advertising, present themselves that actually affects our sense of ourselves as storytellers. If I can get more attention for the kind of shoes I wear or the style of my hair at one-tenth the conscious effort of explaining what the heck is wrong or right about my life in a way that moves you, why bother being a storyteller? Status and recognition, in our consumer culture, is an off-the-rack item.

Finding Your Story

For all these reasons and quite a few others, a persons' initial efforts at story making can be frustrating. We have worked with several high-powered communicators who froze up like a deer in the headlights when it came time for them to construct an emotionally-compelling personal tale.

The starting point for overcoming a creative block is to start with a small idea. It is a natural tendency to want to make a novel or screenplay out of a portion of our life experiences, to think in terms of getting all the details. But it is exactly that kind of scale that disables our memory. Our emphasis on using photographic imagery in our digital storytelling workshops facilitates the process of taking a potential story, picture by picture. Pedro Meyer, in creating his breathtakingly compelling *I Photograph to Remember* CD-ROM, recorded the narrative by simply setting up a tape recorder in his living room. He asked his publisher Bob Stein to sit beside him as he recorded his voice as he described each photograph to Bob. That was it. One take and it became the voice-over that was used for the CD-ROM. This process may work for your project.

Perhaps your project does not originate with visual material on hand. Take a look at our example interview questions in the next section for various kinds of short personal stories. Have someone interview you, then transcribe the words and see what they tell you about the story you are trying to conceive.

As you are working up your raw material for a story, you are also working up your storytelling, or narrative, voice. Everyone has a unique style of expressing

himself or herself that can jump off the page or resonate in a storytelling presentation. Realizing that voice, making it as rich and textured as you are as a
person, takes time and practice.

For many professional communicators, the process of moving from a journalistic or technical, official voice to an organic, natural voice is often difficult. It is
as if we are trying to merge the two different parts of our brains, the analytical
and the emotive. Most of us cannot switch back and forth without getting
dizzy. The official voice is the voice of our expository writing class, of our essays
and term papers, or our formal memos and letters to our professional colleagues. We have been taught that this voice carries dispassionate authority,
useful perhaps in avoiding misunderstandings, but absolutely deadly as a story.

Getting feedback also helps us identify our narrative voice. Reading material to
someone who knows us well, and asking him or her to identify which part is
true to your voice, is a useful practice. Of course, the crafting of the language,
moving away from cliché, eliminating redundancy, and getting out the thesau-
rus to substitute your overused verbs and adjectives, is also important.

Take your time, though, and let the ideas and meanings sink in before you edit.
If something feels overwhelmingly right, do not polish it too much. We have
had lots of scripts that started out fresh and authentic but by the time the
authors and collaborators got through with it, it was filled with succinct, gorgeous, yet characterless, prose. The narrative voice had been polished away.

Interviewing

This series of question sets for the "Interview" or "Self-Interview" process can
assist in the development of different kinds of stories, but it is not meant to
supplant a more direct scripting process if that is how you are accustomed to
working. However, almost all of us can gain from having source material that
appears from an unselfconscious response to a set of directed questions.

By recording your responses, you may find that you have sufficient material to
make your voice-over. Cutting and rearranging your responses using digital
audio editing may be all that is required. If you take this route, keep in mind
that you must take steps to have a good-quality recording.

Interviewing Techniques

You may find it easier to respond to these questions directly into a microphone in the privacy of your own home or office. If the prospect of talking to a recording device is off-putting (and it may be more likely to increase your self-consciousness than relax you), have someone interview you. This could be a friend, a spouse, relative, or co-worker. This process can be both fun and revealing but requires the interviewer commit to a few common-sense ideas.

Guidelines for the Interviewer

First, study the questions so that you are not reading from the page, and feel free to ad lib. Being able to sustain eye contact assists the interviewee in relaxing and responding in a natural way.

Second, allow the interviewee to complete thoughts. Unlike a radio or TV interviewer that is concerned with "dead air" in the conversation, give the interviewee all the time desired to think through and restate something that is a bit difficult to articulate. Interruptions can cause people to lose their train of thought or become self-aware and steer away from important, but perhaps emotionally difficult, information. Let the interviewee tell you when he or she has finished a question before moving on to the next.

Third, when appropriate, use your own intuition to probe further to get a more specific response.

Often people's initial thought about the question only retrieves the broadest outline of memory. Feel free to request specifics or details that would clarify or expand upon a general response.

Fourth, if the story is about information that is specifically painful or traumatic in the persons life, assess carefully how far you allow the respondent to delve into these memories. In many situations where the interviewer is not a spouse or close loved one, you may cross into territory that is much better approached in the context of a purposely therapeutic environment with experienced guides or professionally trained advisors. We have come perilously close in interviews to taking people into an emotional state from which they cannot return at the session. This is embarrassing for the respondent and emotionally inconsiderate, as they may not have the therapeutic support to cope with these issues in the hours and days after the interview. Don't feel you need to hunt for emotionally charged material to make the interview effective. If it comes naturally and comfortably, so be it.

Finally, along with ensuring privacy in the interview, make sure both interviewer and interviewee are comfortable; comfortable chairs, water at hand, and the microphone positioned so not to disrupt ease of movement. (A lavaliere, or pin-on microphone, is the best.)

Kinds of Personal Stories

There are all kinds of stories in our lives that we can develop into multimedia pieces. Here are a few example question sets for some of these stories. Adapting any one of the question sets by integrating sets, or developing a separate set, is encouraged.

The Story About Someone Important

Character Stories

How we love, are inspired by, want to recognize, finding meaning in our relationship to, another person or even pet, is deeply important to us. Perhaps the majority of the stories created in our workshops are about a relationship with a singular other. And in the best of stories they tell us more about ourselves than the details of our own life story.

Memorial Stories

Honoring and remembering people who have passed is an essential part of the process of grieving. While these stories are often the most difficult and painful to produce, the results are the most powerful.

- What is or had been your relationship to this person?
- How would you describe this person (physical appearance, character, etc.)?
- Is there an event/incident that best captures their character?
- What about them do/did you most enjoy?
- What about them drives you crazy?

- What lesson did they give you that you feel is important?
- If you had something to say to them, that they may have never heard you say, what would it be?

The Story About an Event in My Life

Adventure Stories

One of the reasons we travel is that the break from the norm of our lives helps to create vivid memories. All of us who travel, or go on serious adventures, know that the experience is usually an invitation to challenge ourselves, to change our perspective about our lives, to reassess. We often return from these experiences with personal realizations, and the process of recounting our travel stories is as much about sharing those realizations as sharing the sense of beauty or interest in the place visited.

Strangely enough, while almost everyone tells good travel stories, it is often difficult to make an effective multimedia piece from these stories. We rarely think about constructing a story with our photographs or videos in advance of a trip. And we do not want to take ourselves out of the most exhilarating moments by taking out a camera and recording. Before your next trip, think about creating a story outline based on an archetype prior to your visit, and what sorts of images, video, or sounds would be useful to establish the story. That way you can gather some story-related shots at your leisure.

Accomplishment Stories

Accomplishment stories are about achieving a goal, like graduating from school, landing a major contract, or being on the winning team in a sporting event. These stories easily fit into the desire-struggle-realization structure of a classic story. They also tend to be documented, so you might find it easy to construct a multimedia story. Television sports has taken up the accomplishment story as a staple, and it might be helpful for you to look at and deconstruct an "Olympic moment" to see how they balance establishing information, interviews, and voice-over.

- What was the event (time, place, incident, or series of incidents)?
- What was your relationship to the event?
- With whom did you experience this event?

- Was there a defining moment in the event?

- How did you feel during this event (fear, exhilaration, sharpened awareness, joy,...)?

- What did you learn from this event?

- How did this event change your life?

The Story About a Place in My Life

Up until this century, 90% of the world's population was born, lived, and died within a ten-mile radius of their homes. While this is difficult for us to imagine, our sense of place is the basis of many profound stories. One of the earliest interactive storytelling Web sites was a German project, *1,000 Rooms*, that invited people to send a single image of their room at home, and to tell a story about their relationship to their room. Hundreds of people responded with their own intimate stories. You may have a story about your home, an ancestral home, a town, a park, mountain, or forest you love, a restaurant, store, or gathering place. Your insights into place give us insight about your sense of values and connection to community.

- How would you describe the place?

- With whom did you share this place?

- What general experiences do you relate to this place?

- Was there a defining experience at the place?

- What lessons about yourself do you draw from your relationship to this place?

- If you have returned to this place, how has it changed?

The Story About What I Do

Life story for many people in professional careers is shaped by their jobs. Author Studs Terkel collected a series of interviews in his book, *Working*, that demonstrated that we all have unique ways of perceiving and valuing our jobs. For other people, the thing that they do that has most value to them is their hobby or ongoing social commitments. Poignancy often comes from looking at the familiar in a new way, with a new meaning. The details of the tasks, the culture of the characters that inhabit our workplace, our spiritual or philosophical relationship to our work or avocation, lead us into many stories.

- What is your profession or ongoing interest?

- What experiences, interests, and/or knowledge in your previous life prepared you for this activity?

- Was there an initial event that most affected your decision to pursue this interest?

- Who influenced or assisted you in shaping your career, interest, or skill in this area?

- How has your profession or interest affected your life as a whole (family, friends, where you live)?

- What has been the highlight of your vocation/avocation?

Other Personal Stories

Recovery Stories

Sharing the experience of overcoming a great challenge in life, like a health crisis or a great personal obstacle, is the fundamental archetype in human story making. If you can transmit the range of experience from descent, to crisis, to realization, you can always move an audience.

Love Stories

Romance and partnership, familial or fraternal love, also naturally lend themselves to the desire-struggle-realization formula. We all want to know how someone met their partner, what it was like when the baby was born, or what our relationship is with our siblings and parents. We constantly test other people's experiences in these fundamental relationships to affirm our own. These are also stories that tend to have plenty of existing documentation.

Discovery Stories

The process of learning is a rich field to mine for stories. The detective in us gets great pleasure in illustrating how we uncovered the facts to get at the truth, whether it is in fixing a broken bicycle or developing a new product.

As you decide what story would best serve your personal needs, or the needs of your performing or presentation context, keep in mind that these categories are in no way sacrosanct. They cross over in a number of ways. It is also probable that you will come up with your own additional categories or other ways of dissecting the stories in your mind.

Don't Just Sit There...

One of the hardest, but most important thing to do, is getting started. Because many of these stories ask us to reveal things about ourselves that make us feel vulnerable, putting together a story can be a procrastinator's paradise. Just get up, start answering questions on a tape recorder, write things down, gather up the photos, review your videos, and bounce your ideas around your friends and family.

Life is full of stories, but you may not have a lifetime to capture them as movies. So, go for it!

4 Approaches to the Scripting Process

Prompts and Processes

After the first year of offering Digital Storytelling Workshops in 1994, Nina and I saw the need to closely examine how people approached the writing process for their digital stories. Just because the subject matter was clear to a workshop participant, it wasn't always easy to get the script written. In the last chapter we talked about some of the reasons for that, but we really didn't discuss the notion of how to find your best creative voice for expressing yourself in writing. In the next chapter, I'll talk about form and structure for your story, as well as the considerations for working in multiple media, so leave aside those considerations for the moment. I am talking about how writing happens, and what makes the way you write unique and powerful.

Our own practice has suggested several methods for success. We have also attempted to stay up to date with our colleagues' efforts in the broader field of creative writing and personal storytelling. In the bibliography, we reference a number of highly effective books on writing personal stories that we have used in our curriculum at UC Berkeley and as companions to some of our projects in the field.

As with our approach to digital storytelling in general, we find our practice is ideally suited to group settings. You could use these ideas to get started on your own, but success happens as often by comparing your work to others, and by hearing a variety of examples. So find a few friends, declare yourself a writer's group, gather once a week for a month and share your writing. Your digital story will thank you for your efforts.

Our Friend, the 4 x 6 Index Card

Of all the suggestions that we have made in helping people to prepare their writing, the use of 4 x 6 index cards has garnered the most praise.

The idea is simple. Writers, both novice and established, inevitably suffer from the malady aptly called "blank page syndrome." The weight of filling a blank page, or more likely many pages, crushes our creative initiative, and so, we cannot get going. It is not only how to start, but the overwhelming sense of the stack of blank paper, notebook, or endless word processing scroll that needs to be filled that makes the task seem undoable.

In our workshops, when we have found a person looking at the word processor with the deer-in-the-headlights look in their eye, we hand them a 4 x 6 index card. We say either, "you have 10 minutes, and only the space on the front and back of this card, to create a draft of your story. Write whatever comes out and don't stop until either the time or the card runs out." Or we say, "This is a postcard. Choose a person that you think this story is for, and write them a postcard about the story. Start with Dear _____."

The card is small. It is finite. It seems possible, perhaps even easy to fill. So for the novice, it is saying just get this much down, and we'll work from there. For writers confident of their ability write pages with their prose, it is also a creative challenge. We know you could write a novel, now just try and say it in only this much space.

One of my favorite Mark Twain quotes is from his sending a letter to a friend. He wrote, "Forgive me, this is a long letter. I would have written you a short letter, but I didn't have the time." Shorter isn't always easier for the mature writer.

The 4 x 6 card condenses the narrative as well. What are you choices in beginning? How quickly must you get into the action of the narrative? Usually this means sacrificing the long exposition that usually accompanies the first draft of a story. But often that works, particularly in a story that is narrating a visual narrative.

And finally, we are very, very pleased by short and effective digital stories. If the writing is no longer than the front and back of a 4 x 6 card (about 1 double spaced typed page), it insures that the writing will lead to a two to three minute story when narrated. Just the right size.

Writing Exercises

In a group process, I am a big fan of writing exercises. While I am fully aware of the potential and beauty of free writing, have the class spend ten to twenty minutes writing down whatever comes to their head. I find the shared themes and ideas of a prompted idea connects people to each other in wonderful ways.

This is my favorite prompt:

> *In our lives, there are moments, decisive moments, when the direction of our lives was pointed in a given direction, and because of the events of this moment, we are going in another direction. Poet Robert Frost shared this concept simply as The Road Not Taken. The date of a major achievement, the time there was a particularly bad setback, meeting a special person, the birth of a child, the end of a relationship, the death of a loved one, are all examples of these fork-in-the-road experiences. Right now, at this second, write about a decisive moment in your life. You have 10 minutes.*

The writing that comes from this prompt, when it comes unannounced at the beginning of a workshop, often goes straight to an emotional heart of the author's life. The sharing of these kinds of stories can be instantly bonding for a group. And once in awhile, they lead to new ideas for the digital story that the participant has brought to the class.

If the goal is to prod distant memories, we have not found a better approach than Bill Roorbach's idea of having participants in the workshop first draw a map of the neighborhood where they grew up (*Writing Life Stories*, Story Press, 1998 pp.21-34). Reaching back in one's memory to locate the layout of the streets, where friends lived, the names of friendly or weird neighbors, the way to the store, or the secret paths to school, inevitably opens up a hundred possible stories. The physicalization of a memory, trying to remember a time by remembering the places of that time, places you traveled through on a daily basis, a neighborhood, a house, a room, usually leads quickly to events, events that are rich with the kinds of meaningful inspections that make good stories.

There are innumerable prompts that might work for various situations. Here is a short list of some themes for which prompts could also be built for powerful stories. Books about writing are filled with these exercises, so don't forget to pick up a few when it's time to look deeper into your interest in writing beyond the digital storytelling experience.

- Tell the story of a mentor or hero in your life.

- Tell the story of a time when "it just didn't work"—a point, at your job, or at an activity at which you are competent or are usually successful, when everything fell apart before your eyes.

- Describe a time when you felt really scared.

- Tell the story of a "first"—first kiss, first day on a job, first time trying something really difficult, the first time your heard a favorite song, etc.

- And of course, the old standby, what was the most embarrassing thing that ever happened to you?

These Stories from These Pictures

Digital stories often start with the pictures. Our easiest direction to anyone thinking about making a digital story is to look around their house, on the mantle, or the old shoebox, and find some images that provoke stories. Then see if there are other images around the house that are part of that story.

As we talk about storyboarding and structure, the notion of the illustration of the script is emphasized as an outgrowth of the successful drafting of your narration. But we would guess that 20 percent of the people that have come to the workshop have taken the absolutely opposite approach to the process. They pull out the photos, arrange them on a table, and then sort out an order from beginning to end. With the story visually organized, they then start writing. Is this effective? Of course. Some great stories have emerged through this process.

Our only caveat is to consider whether or not by responding to the images alone, you are possibly leaving out parts of a story that never were captured in any images in your archive. If you do imagine an image that is missing, then you can look to an illustration or appropriately implicit or metaphorical representation to capture the sense of the writing.

Getting into the Scene

When authors come to the Digital Storytelling Workshop, we have them share first drafts or just talk about their ideas for the story. The feedback will sometimes reference the ideas in structure that are discussed in the first three of the Seven Elements (see Chapter 5), but often I find myself discussing the notion of scene with the authors.

As an example, I can take one approach to my own story about my father's death.

> *Well, first of all, let me just say, I was seventeen at the time. And I had finished high school that summer. My dad had smoked three packs a day, and had been trying to quit smoking for a couple of months. He was 61, and had a difficult life as a union organizer working in Texas and the South. But we had had a vacation the month before and he seemed like he was doing okay.*
>
> *He came down from his bedroom saying that he had a terrible pain. We called the doctor. The doctor said that it was probably an ulcer attack. He had had several of those. We waited. He got much worse. We decided to rush him to the hospital. It was a heart attack. He died within a half hour. My mom was hysterical. It was a night I will always remember.*

What we have is a fairly typical set of expository contexts and sequence of events that most people use to casually recall a major catastrophe in their lives. It is a fairly direct, and distanced recitation of the facts. And it usually finishes with a statement that is conclusive, but as in this example, understated and obvious to the extreme. If this was dramatic dialogue, a speech by an actor pretending to be natural, it would be fine.

But here is a description of the same memory that I shared at my mother's memorial in 2001, twenty-seven years after my father died. This is how my statement began.

> *I will never forget the sound of my mom's voice when the doctor said, "George is dead."*
>
> *God No! No! No!.*
>
> *A scream. A release. An explosion.*

The sound of her wail bounced off all the walls of the emergency room at Presbyterian Hospital in Dallas, bounced down the streets and through the trees, bounced out into the night sky, all the way across the universe of my young mind.

In a single moment, a single pronouncement, everything changed for my mom. It divided her life in two. And it taught me that love can reach down into the cellular essence of awareness, and with its rupture, tear a human being in half.

What differentiates these two texts for me is, in the second text, that I am asking my audience to immediately journey in time with me to the exact instant when it all really happened. No context, other than the assumption that "George" must be someone really important, and the feelings, best as I remembered them, of the defining moment of the experience, my mom's reaction to the Doctor's words. And finally, with over 25 years perspective, what that means to me now.

I tried to take the audience into the scene at the hospital. I could have described the way it looked and smelled, where we were standing moments before the doctor came up, what happened afterwards, but I assumed that when I said it is the moment that my father was pronounced dead. Instead it serviced my sense of the writing to strip away all this descriptive material.

We have found that audiences really can build a fairly elaborate guess as to the pre-text of an event. And we know that much of what seems like important background, is in fact superfluous to what really happened and what it really felt like to be there.

Taking the audience to the moment of an important scene, one that either initiates or concludes your tale, and putting them in your shoes, is why we listen to the story. We want to know how characters react. We want to imagine ourselves there as participants or witnesses. We want to know what someone else takes away from the experience, and uses to lead their lives forward.

This idea of scene is related but separate from the terms of the specific disciplines of literature, theater and film. Dramatic scenes all have complex sets of conventions that allow us to observe the action of characters within a continuous time of the narrative. In our thinking about scene, all we want is to encourage people to share at least one portion of their narrative as a scene—to write as if they were there, inside the events as they unfolded, experiencing their shock, surprise, amusement, etc, for the first time. For many stories, this strips away the superficial consideration of the events, and gets to the heart of the matter.

Character Studies and Personal Story

We know that most of our parents are multi-faceted, complex humans. In one story, it may serve to have the parent in the classic role of the ideal mentor, filling one stereotype of parenthood. In another story, the parent may be a beast, or display beastly behavior, but if we are mature enough, and we are given one small nugget of context, for example, "when they got drunk, they would be mean," it is sufficient for us to imagine they had good days as well. We are probably aware that the story is a cautionary tale about human behavior, not the evidence to indict the guilty party.

Lagos Egri, author of the bible of my training in dramatic theory, *The Art of Dramatic Writing*, (Touchstone Books; February 1972), reduced all great storytelling, all great theater, to the author's understanding of the true nature of the characters he invents in the world of his narrative. Like most people, when I watch a film or a play, it stops working the moment I say to myself, "you know, that character would have never said those words, or behaved in that way." In any story, it simply will not work if both characters strengths and flaws do not drive the series of events forward leading logically to the climactic clash or coming together that delivers the conclusion of the story.

When we write in the first person, about real events, about real people, we make the same choices as the fictional author, that is to share description of the characters only as is pertinent to the story. It is nothing short of egomaniacal to imagine these characters are faithful portraits of the actual people. In our digital stories, they are not even sketches, more like cartoons or line drawings.

Some of the writers that have participated in our workshops are a bit fixated about faithfulness in their study of character. They fear providing too simplistic a picture of the people they are describing, or their behavior in a given context, so they expand the narrative with a multiplicity of facets in the endeavor to feel more "fair." Personal storytellers are not judges or juries, they are witnesses, and just as with witnesses we seek truth inside and around the simple lines of the sketch of their memories. We, the audience, are capable of judging from their approach to the narrative, if their attitude and tone reflect balanced judgment or unreasonable accusation.

By letting the story dictate the degree to which we need to know the background of the character, we avoid cluttering some of the prose with assessments that cancel each other out. Why is certain behavior typical or surprising, for example. Which characteristic, for the purpose of the story, can we fill in with the broad brush of a stereotype sufficient for our small tale so the audience can fill out the character with the complexities of their own experience with specific individuals.

Finally, A Few Words on Style

During my high school and early college days as a young journalist, I carried around a copy of *Elements of Style*, the William Strunk and E.B. White companion for all writers. I have to be frank, except for their call for economy, economy, economy, not much stuck in my sense of the rules of good style. In other words, I am the last person to teach anyone about formal issues of style.

Having said that, Strunk and White might have been apoplectic at much of what I love in the styles of the writing of our students. What works, particularly as the words leave the page and are spoken by the authors, is not a case study in language usage according to conventions of grammar and syntax defended by the gatekeepers of the English (or any other) language.

What works is truth. What I mean is a given author's truth about how they conceive of their way of telling a story. How does truth happen in storytelling? Here is where the journey metaphor serves me best. Good writing has a destination, and seeks the shortest path to the destination, but no shorter. The destination, as we discuss in the next chapter, is usually the punch line, the pay-off, the point of the story. Detours are never accidental, unconscious, or indulgent. Each word, each apparent digression, is critical to the final resolution of the characters' action. I am a traditionalist in this idea, having never fallen for what feels to me a experimentalist conceit of an anything goes approach to narrative.

But that is my truth. I have had the pleasure of hearing thousands of people share their stories, each with their own style of telling. Some people like the journey along the road of their story and a bunch of learning that happens along the way, rather the arrival of a singular big lesson or moral to the story. Other people love the wonderful mystery and elasticity of language, and what they mean by story is what I might mean by poetry. Other people find themselves hearing the sounds of words like music, and really are not concerned with meaning of the words per se as much as the aural jazz of the presentation that creates a dominant tonal impression whose meaning is profoundly more complex than the simple "message" of the story. In that sense, I accept that when it works, it works.

The good news about those of us living at the beginning of the twenty-first century is that we have an awareness that what and how we tell our stories has much less impact than how we are heard. Stories do a number of things to people, but only a small part of what they do has to do with our intention with the style and content of the story. When people hear the story, what is going on in their lives at that moment that focuses or distracts their attention, what ways the story is contextualized where the story is being heard, the ambiance of the environment, who else is in the audience, etc., changes everything about the story and its impact.

We felt this in our own workshops when the fabulous release of the completion of a workshop and the enormously transformative effect each story has on all of the participants cannot possibly translate to an audience that did not share our story circle.

So trust your own voice, the way it feels right to you to put things, and your own approach to these stories. And make sure, that when it comes time to share your story, you are certain that the context is best suited to your story being appreciated at its fullest.

Interlude Two

Burning Memories

What can we say about our grandmothers? That they were nice to us, that they sang to us, that they smelled of juicy fruit and Pond's cold cream and watched the "Wheel of Fortune." That they wrapped everything in plastic baggies and pinched our thighs.

What about what they did to our mothers? Mine was always so sweet to me but I remember the time when Mom and I met her at the airport and before she sat down her valise, she looked my mom up and down and said "you know Debbie, you'd be very pretty if you had larger breasts."

My mom was almost 40 years old.

Years later, we talked about it. My mom would try to laugh some and say that her mother, my grandmother, was crazy.

"Your feet are too bony…"
"You look like a stick…"
"No man is going to want that…"
"You should wear falsies, like I do…"

She would beat her with a hair brush and drag her around the house by her braids… After one such event, my mother went into the bathroom, took a pair of scissors from the medicine cabinet and cut them off.

We sat on the couch and tried to figure out how not to care so much about what our mothers said. She showed me her high school picture. We looked at it and I told her how beautiful she was.

She had never known.

This spring my mother and I are going to the California coast

We are going to take the doll my grandmother always compared her to…

And burn it.

Falsies
—Daniel Weinshenker

Once in awhile I am stunned by the simple first reading of a script.

We were sitting around the table in our small lab at UC Berkeley in the Fall of '99 with the usual odd assortment of participants, a preacher from Portland, a drag queen from SF, a couple of elementary school teachers and three representatives of a dot.com company. We are heading around the table and this cool looking dot.com dude from Colorado sheepishly introduces himself. "I am not really a visual guy, and the script is bit short, and …" The normal list of excuses.

Then he reads. Wow.

The quality of his delivery was part of the impact, he knew how to read, and I was not surprised to find Daniel was both trained as and considered himself a poet. But there was something else, a sense of release in the way the words and ideas reveal themselves. It was also some old-fashioned courage.

The finished digital story was even more effective. He made it sing.

As I have shared this piece, I have seen a wave of recognition cross people's faces. They remember their own losses. Their own disappointments. The worse kind of injury, the ones that leave the deepest scar…because it came from someone they most loved.

We all have stories like these. We really must share them. Or we cannot heal.

5 Seven Elements

Story Structure and Design in Digital Storytelling

There are many kinds of stories, and many ways to find your creative voice as a storyteller, but it is almost impossible to imagine the number of ways a single story can be structured. And, when you factor in the choices of the filmmaker; in design of visual elements and audio, in thinking about how the story is performed and paced, and what is possible in the world of computer-generated effects, we are talking about an infinite variety of expression.

Fortunately, the participants in our classes arrive with an enormous range of skills and life experience that suggests a particular path of individual style and structure to their story. Our role as digital storytelling facilitators is to coach a storyteller past the particular roadblocks they face. Story coaching is a dynamic process, not a prescribed one. An entire range of issues must be considered while offering suggestions, both technical and emotional. There are as many ways as there are people in which to do this.

When we succeed in providing the right sort of feedback to the creator, we often witness an extraordinary transformation in the quality of story. It is gratifying for us as teachers to bring a new story to life. To see the eyes of the creator well up with tears of surprise and joy at what he or she has accomplished, and to see others moved and inspired by the power of the piece, is what keeps us going, class after class.

The seven elements evolved after teaching our workshops for a couple of years. We decided to introduce each class to the elements of constructing a multimedia story. Between the emotional fragility of exploring a personal issue, and feelings of inadequacy when working with computers or multimedia, the last thing our students needed was someone dictating a specific formula to them. So we kept it simple. Illustrating our few points with examples of student work from previous classes, our principal consideration was to make it brief and inspirational.

The seven elements we describe in the pages that follow give you a great deal to consider in constructing your story. We emphasize our storytelling process in group settings because we believe that most people do not just read a book and then do the work. Storytelling is meant to be a collaborative art. It is much more realistic this way, and much more fun.

1. Point (of View)

What makes a story a story? Dictionary definitions may call it a narrative, a tale, a report, an account, and that would seem to cover it.

But hold on. When we think of a story, true or imagined, we do not consider someone sitting in front of us reciting a series of events like a robot: "This happened, then this happened, and then this happened." Hardly anyone narrates events in their lives without some good reason.

We believe all stories are told to make a point. Most stories follow the pattern of describing a desire, a need, or a problem that must be addressed by a central character. They follow the action the desire leads us to take, and then reveal realizations or insights that occurred as a result of experiencing the events of our actions and their relationship to our original desire. By point of view, we primarily are addressing this issue of defining the specific realization you, as an author, are trying to communicate within your story. Because every part of the story can service this point, it becomes imperative to define this goal in order to direct the editing process.

We need to look no further than proverbs to illustrate what we mean by a point of view. "A stitch in time saves nine." "A penny wise and a pound foolish." These are the points of stories, what somebody realized was the actual result, versus the desired effect, of a planned action. We may have forgotten the stories, but we remember the point. In novels or theater, another way of expressing the point of the story is the central premise. For example, in *King Lear*, the point or central premise is "blind trust leads to destruction." In *Macbeth*, it is "unbridled greed leads to destruction." Every part of the dramatic action can be boiled down to serving these points of view, and our connection with the story often succeeds or fails in how we understand the central premise as the operating context for the story's action. In well-crafted stories, the point may be a little less apparent than the moral of a fairy tale, and it might require some thought, but if the story touched you, chances are you can define some central points or the transformative realizations the author intended.

Example

In 1994, we assisted on a project called *The Answer*, created by the husband-and-wife team of Rob Decker and Suzanne Serpas. They were both psychologists with an interest in the potential of autobiography as a therapeutic tool. They came to us with a large box of stock commercial images and an ambitious concept to provide a metaphoric look at the importance of a humanist perspective on the world, a kind of commercial for their brand of psychotherapy. We felt that they had defined their subject so broadly that they would not be able to complete the project over the weekend. We also felt that their personal connection to the point of the story was lost. We suggested they narrow the subject and asked if they had an example of the kind of realization they wanted their audience to experience. Rob subsequently offered the story that became the script of the final piece:

> *The other day I asked my 7-year-old daughter about the meaning of life. "Well," she answered without hesitation, "there's having fun, having love in your family, and learning things, you know, knowledge." I spent 49 years searching for the meaning of life. I guess I should have had the good sense to ask a kid in the first place.*

They simply juxtaposed Rob reciting the story with the standard family images and home video and voila: a powerful little tale about their realization about how we define our essential human values from an early age.

In thinking about the point of a story, we should also be considering the reason for the story. Why this story, now, for this group of people? Defining these issues inevitably helps to define which of the many proverbial summations we might take from a given story.

Let's imagine a fairly typical process of developing a story, and the struggle to define point of view.

> *Esperanza has decided to make a story about her non-profit organization, Familias Unidas, a community organization assisting low-income Latino families with negotiating the social service systems.*

From the organizational brochure, and from all the grant proposals she has written, she has a great deal of argumentation about why her organization exists and why it deserves continued community support. She also has 10 years of images of work with community members, special events, staff members, and the several times the organization has been recognized with awards.

But as she thinks about the purpose of her story, she realizes the mission statement and lists of achievements do not really capture the emotional essence of what they do. If the digital story is going to be presented to their supporters at the Christmas fundraiser and then get put on the website, it needs to move people, not just present a list of activities and goals and objectives.

What she decides is to create a portrait of one of the families they have helped. Esperanza has always liked the profiles of community service she has seen on television. She knows just the family, the Sanchez family. She goes to meet with them, and they are interested. But as they talk about the role of Familias Unidas in their lives, Esperanza realizes their story only touches on one or two of the half dozen programs the organization offers. She needs several families to capture a broad enough point of view about the organization to connect with the different stakeholders in her communities of support. This is so much work. "This will never get done," Esperanza thinks. She is the director of the program, and as it is, she barely has time to work on the project.

That night, she speaks with her partner, Carolina, who laughs about how Esperanza is always getting overwhelmed. "Just like how you started the whole thing, fresh out of college, full of ideals, you start helping a few friends of your cousin get some paperwork turned in for the local clinic, and the next thing you were helping everyone in the vecino (neighborhood). You hardly slept then." Esperanza remembered these times, and how passionate she felt, and how her passion inspired others to take up this work, and to give donations to support it. Maybe that's the story, not just what we do, but why we do it, how caring starts with just one person. She calls her cousin and asks if he would be willing to tell the story of those first projects. He says he would be honored. She starts writing, and the words flow. From this beginning story she connects the

Sanchez family's experience to show how the program became professionalized, and she finishes with a reflection on her own growth and the gifts that this work has given her.

At midnight, she closes her laptop. Esperanza sees the movie playing in her head. "I know just the images to use," she says to herself. On the desk next to her computer, she has an ofrenda, an altar, to her grandmother. Just as she lights the candle, as she does each night before bed, she feels a light puff of air blow from over her shoulder. She looks back. Nothing.

A breath? An affirmation.

Maybe Esperanza got more than her name from her abuelita (grandmother).

From this story, you can see how the process of defining premise is both demanding and enlightening. We have seen in project after project, workshop participants struggling for that particular clarity of purpose, having the insight come to them at the last moment, and the piece practically editing itself once they find the ideal point of view.

The story of Esperanza also illustrates another perspective we have on Point of View. We believe all stories are personal. For most storytellers, couching the story in the first-person point of view, either throughout the story or as a frame around the story, is an invitation to hearing the story in a more personal context. This tends to increase our attention as we look for insights about you as a storyteller. That is, "This is my version of events and my realizations, and I am self-aware about how my own prejudices, expertise, and frames of reference affect the 'truth' about the story."

We, as information consumers, are becoming increasingly sophisticated at discerning the authenticity of information. In general, we prefer the frank admission of responsibility that the first-person voice provides to the authoritative, seemingly neutral, but nevertheless obscure stance of the third-person voice.

In our workshops, we have advised against the brochure-ware approach to narrative associated with a business language, bureaucrateze or "grant-speak" that is endemic in our culture. When possible, the person making the story should find their own connection to the material. If an organization wants to capture the stories of their clients, consumers, staff members, then they should invite those stakeholders to write and create their own digital stories.

2. Dramatic Question

Simply making a point doesn't necessarily keep people's attention throughout a story. Well-crafted stories, from Shakespeare to Seinfeld, set up a tension from the beginning that holds you until the story is over.

In Tristane Rainer's *Your Life As Story*, she reduces all stories to a desire-action-realization model. For her, a story establishes a central desire in the beginning in such a way that the satisfaction or denial of that desire must be resolved in order for the story to end. The conflicts that arise between our desires being met and the desire of other characters or larger forces to stop us create the dramatic tension.

Dramatic and storytelling theorists, anthropologists, philosophers, and psychologists since the time of Aristotle have attempted to analyze how the action of a story is established and sustained. We have found that delineating structural story components for students who are essentially working in a short narrative form is much too complicated. Writing a script that slavishly follows a formal structure tends to create wooden, melodramatic writing that we can smell a mile off as not reflecting the author's true voice. So we have reduced these several concepts to one.

We refer to a term coined from dramatic theory, "the dramatic question," to summarize an approach. In a romance, will the girl get the guy? In an adventure, will the hero reach the goal? In a crime or murder mystery, who did it? When any of these questions are answered, the story is over.

Again, sophisticated story making distinguishes itself by burying the presentation of the dramatic question, like the realization, in ways that do not call attention to the underlying structure.

In Interlude One, we talked about Monte Hallis' *Tanya*. It remains one of the most poignant and efficient expressions of digital storytelling we have experienced and has also served as an ideal example of a number of the elements we are currently describing, particularly the dramatic question.

The statement of the dramatic question is elegantly posed and resolved in the first and closing lines. Monte states at the beginning that she didn't understand friendship. At the end she leaves us with a rather open-ended statement, "I couldn't believe she knew my middle name." It does not take much sophistication to interpret the dramatic question, "What is the meaning of friendship?" The answer suggests that it is the ways in which we unconsciously exchange intimate information with each other.

In this case, the particular meaning of the resolution of the dramatic question is in fact the central point of the story. But here is an important distinction. What we are really talking about with the dramatic question is a structural "setup," corresponding to a logical "payoff." The meaning of the story, as we have suggested, doesn't have to have anything to do with the structure, just as there are hundreds of ways to draw different meanings out of any given sequence of events.

We are trained from early on to recognize that different dramatic questions often lead to predictable answers. If the question is about how the girl gets the guy, our immediate assumption is that either the guy, or someone the guy knows, doesn't want the guy to be gotten. As a result, manipulating expectations is precisely what entertains us. What if the girl thinks she wants one guy, but she really wants the guy who is trying to stop her from getting the original guy? What if she decides to chuck the whole thing and become a nun? Are we unhappy? Only if there was nothing to suggest that these events were consistent with her behavior will we be confused or dismayed. A good author will make you think the central dramatic question was "Will the girl get the guy?" when it really was "Will the girl find happiness?" and we have learned early on that she doesn't define herself completely by her role as spousal partner. If you watch movies, you know the possibilities for manipulating the dramatic question are endless.

When we have the expectation pulled out from under us in a story, when the realization is dramatically different than the setup, it tickles us. The classic short story does the same, leading us quickly into a direction that establishes our expectations, only to twist the expectation at the end.

The more you learn about dramatic structure, the more you dissect familiar stories into their structural components. The more you experiment with rewarding or surprising your audience's expectations as sparked by a dramatic question, the more rich and complex your stories will become.

3. Emotional Content

All of us have been in the middle of a story, a novel, a film, a theatrical or story-telling performance and found ourselves emotionally engaged. It is as if the story had reached inside our consciousness and taken hold of us, and we know in that moment that we are in for a tearful or joyous ride.

This effect is principally a result of a truthful approach to emotional material. A story that deals directly with the fundamental emotional paradigms—of death and our sense of loss, of love and loneliness, of confidence and vulnerability, of acceptance and rejection—will stake a claim on our hearts. Beginning with content that addresses or couches itself in one or another of those contexts will improve the likelihood that you are going to hold an audience's attention.

One of the fundamental ways to understand story's role in our lives is to think of most stories as resurrection tales. A character must know a negation of their desire in order to finally achieve their desire. In the tragic form, the protagonist is usually destroyed in order that other characters, and we the audience, can understand the consequence of the fatal flaw of the character, and/or the poignant power of circumstance/fate. In the comic form, love must certainly be lost at some point, for us to feel great satisfaction of the final hoped for embrace. The hero must be on the very edge of extinction before victory or the goal of the quest is achieved.

Why is this so powerful? On one level, every one of us has to wake up in the morning, and choose to go on, to resurrect ourselves in the face of fate and circumstance, the memory of loss and almost unbearable struggle, and our own sense of weakness and vulnerability. The stories we are drawn to, that resonate in our direct emotional need, in general, are those that give us a reason to make the decision to go forward. They inspire us. The very word inspire, in its archaic meaning, is to breathe again. Stories encourage us to take one more breath, to swim up to the surface, above our despair, and live.

We believe all stories can have an element of these emotional paradigms. Even our story about Esperanza's trying to get her own story together for her organization, had the potential of negation. She almost gave up, having become overwhelmed with the problem of achieving her goal. When you look at the story you want to tell, think about where in the story was the possibility that what was desired—a happy vacation, success in the project, understanding in a relationship—can be contrasted with its opposite—a rainy, nasty day on the beach, a disastrous change in plans, a painful argument. How we get past the hard part, and still get what we desire, this is what we want to know.

For many of us these areas are a challenge to express in a piece of personal writing or media. We may lack the experience of trying, as most if not all of our formal training processes in narrative—from scholarly essays to journalistic reports—stress distance and de-emotionalized perspectives. Or we may be unresolved about the emotional material, keeping us from gaining perspective or meaning from these experiences. The result of our failure to express our most honest understandings about these kinds of subject matter can lead us to trivialize or over dramatize the material. It can also lead us to being simply overwhelmed by feelings that are brought to the surface.

Is it worth the effort to expose oneself emotionally? In most cases, it is. In our experience with the group production process, people value the courage to explore the intimate space of emotional vulnerability so highly that they will go out of their way to support those willing to attempt emotionally sensitive stories. But sometimes we are forced to steer students away from overpowering material, to select a different approach, or abandon the subject of the story entirely. This part of digital storytelling requires plain old-fashioned common sense and maturity.

Along these lines, many people who read this may want to experiment with teaching or leading workshops as a way to mine powerful stories from a group of associates for the purposes of linking those emotions to a product, cause, or service. This may be quite effective, but can also be exploitative.

We want to emphasize that exploring emotional material is a personal decision. Our workshops are based on the idea of creating a safe place for people to share stories. Protecting and honoring the trust of the workshop is a central tenet of the work. That safety cannot be extended to broadcast or publication, or to all potential audiences. Unexpected reactions, innocent or malevolent interpretations that disrespect the author's intent are possible once the work is released to a broad audience. Thinking through the degree of your emotional vulnerability in shaping the point of view of the story, in regards to audience, is always important.

4. The Gift of Your Voice

In our classes we encourage the storyteller to record a voiceover. Students may want to make a piece with only images and music, and some are working on stories that they feel are best suited to a particular voiceover or character representation. What we have learned in this process is in itself revealing.

I grew up with a lisp. When I was seven or eight, I had to go to speech therapy classes thso I wouldn't thspeak thso listhpisthly. Like most kids, it made me hate the way my voice sounded. That didn't stop me from being the class clown and being the ham in the school productions, or perhaps it emboldened me. But when I first ran into a tape recorder, I couldn't stand the way I sounded. And frankly, it still bothers me.

Having worked with a lot of people who are creating a piece of video that includes their voice for the first time, I realize I am not alone. Either we feel we don't have the clearest diction, or our voices waver, or we are too soft, or too gravelly, or just not like those caramel-textured assertive voices that come across our television sets and radios.

Truly, our voice is a great gift. Those of us fortunate enough to be able to talk out loud should love our voices, because they tell everyone so much about who we are, both how strong we can be and how fragile.

We listen to words spoken in various inflections and go into different modes of listening, which are also different modes of conscious interaction. When we hear conversational tones, we are listening for the moment that suggests response or affirmation, the "Oh I agree, but..." or the "hm-hmm." In a speech we are listening for an applause line. In a lecture, we are listening for the major points, the outline. In a story, we are listening for an organic rhythmic pattern that allows us to float into reverie. In the place of reverie we have a complex interaction between following the story and allowing the associative memories the story conjures up to wash over us. Consistency in presentation is what allows us in the audience to participate, and breaking consistency, such as a person who is reciting a monologue suddenly asking someone in the front row a question, is jarring.

We have one specific concern to address about recording our voices: reading versus reciting the script. We all know what it feels like to be at a public event when someone reads a speech from beginning to end. It is downright uncomfortable. We do not know how to interact. We are caught someplace between waiting for the speaker to give pause for us to respond and wanting to drift into reverie, but the cadence and style of presentation does not allow it. We also know why people end up reading texts. They are petrified to speak and/or they simply do not have the time to practice the speech enough so that they can recite from memory. Similarly, in recording a voiceover from a script in our workshops, there usually is a combination of fear and lack of time for practice that means a reading seems like the only option.

The easiest way to improve upon a recording of your voice is to keep the writing terse. Record several takes of the text. The nice thing about a digital sound file is that you can mix and match each of the recording takes to create the best-sounding version. We suggest you work at speaking slowly in a conversational style. Finally, digitally constructing the story from a recorded interview is always a good fallback.

5. The Power of the Soundtrack

In our experience working with beginning students, their intuitive sense of what music is appropriate for a media piece is by far their most developed skill in the storytelling arts. In an era where we describe an entire generation as "the children of MTV," as people defined by their absorption of visual media in the context of music, is it any real surprise?

We have come to believe that people now walk around with soundtracks running in their heads. Those soundtracks set the mood of our day, change the way we perceive the visual information streaming into our eyes, and establish a rhythm for our step. It is as if by listening to or imagining a specific slice of music, we are putting ourselves into our own movie, a movie that puts our life into a clearer perspective, or at least entertains us.

From earlier and earlier ages we are aware of the trick that music can play on our perception of visual information. We are all aware of how music in a film stirs up an emotional response very different than what the visual information inherently suggests. The sudden opening of the door becomes the prelude to disaster, when the swelling treble of orchestrated strings calls out suspense to our ears. A sweetly flowing melody over two people looking at each other for the first time signals that these are the romantic characters we will be following in the plot. We know upbeat music means happy endings, slow and tremulous music means sadness is forecast, fast music means action, heroic music means battles and victorious heroes are likely. We know the stereotype, and it is repeated enough from one show to the next that we often laugh when we catch ourselves being caught up in the manipulation. As such, even the beginning student makes appropriate decisions about music that either play into or against the stereotype.

The majority of our students use popular lyrical music. While the songs usually work, mistakes are sometimes made in mixing the lyrical story of the song and the voiceover narrative in a way that gives us an unintended conflict of meaning. I remember a young student who liked a particular song that had an appropriate tempo and timbre for his story about his family, but in listening a bit more to the lyrics, we realized the song was a fairly steamy account of passion. We asked if that was intended and the student admitted that he had not really thought about what was being said in the song.

Instrumental music, whether classical, folk, jazz, or ambient, is often better suited to the style and meaning of the story's text and visual narratives. The digital context makes testing a particular music in the video much easier than in film and analog media, and so experimentation is encouraged. You may find that, by going against the expected, you create another complete layer of meaning that adds depth and complexity to your story.

Are music videos, or the juxtaposition of music and visual information in a media piece without text and voiceover, storytelling? The answer is yes. However, the specificity of language and the complexity of information that the human voice provides adds enormous emotional substance and authenticity to the media story. So far we have not experienced a single music video that created as powerful an emotional impact as the same story would have with the addition of the author's voice.

The other area of sound use popular in the film and video tradition is sound effects and other elements of sound design beyond the mix of music and text. There is no question that the greater design of ambient sound or appropriate noises can add complexity to the narrative. They also can be juxtaposed to add surprise and humor. The development of these skills should be considered if the storytelling projects call for an increased sense of realism or, for that matter, surrealism. Otherwise, it is perhaps best not to experiment with sound effects, as their incidental use is usually more of a distraction.

Using your own voice and existing personal image and moving image archival material has the advantage of being copyrighted by you as the author. By using other's music, you are also likely crossing into the territory of deciding what should be the appropriate fair use of the copyrighted material. Put simply, if you are going to make money directly or indirectly by the presentation or distribution of the piece you have created, then you should have the composer's permission to use the music. Fortunately, numerous companies have developed copyright-free music collections and software to assist you in designing a soundtrack that is wholly yours. Finding a friend to play a piano or strum a guitar can also solve this problem. Be creative.

6. Economy

Economy is generally the largest problem with telling a story. Most people do not realize that the story they have to tell can be effectively illustrated with a small number of images and video, and a relatively short text. We purposely put limitations on the number of images and video clips used by our students. We also suggest that, if they are starting with a script, they create a storyboard with their material and look at every possible way to edit their words prior to beginning the production process.

Despite our emphasis on story, multimedia for many storytellers is principally a visual medium that integrates the other elements. As a visual medium we are concerned with composition and juxtaposition of visual elements in a single screen and over time. Since our emphasis is in repurposing existing images and video, your initial compositional considerations were already decided by your relative skill in shooting a picture or framing a video. Our concern is more with sequential composition.

In any story we use a process called closure. Closure means recognizing the pattern of information being shown or described to us in bits and pieces, and completing the pattern in our minds.

In spoken word or a written narrative, we are operating at a high level of closure as we are filling in all the pictures suggested by a text or words from images and memories in our brains. If I start a story, "Once upon a midnight dreary..." you are likely to immediately fill in a mental image of a foreboding castle, rainstorms, ravens, the works. We need specific sensual details, shapes, smells, and textures to be stated for us to fill in the picture in our mind.

Storytelling with images means consciously economizing language in relationship to the narrative that is provided by the juxtaposition of images. There are two tracks of meaning, the visual and the auditory, and we need to think about the degree of closure each provides in relation to the other. In a normal screen-writing process, the writer is conscious of the visual information as the context for the spoken dialogue or narration, and he or she writes into the visual back-drop of the scenes. If the writer and director do a good job, they will shoot just what is necessary to keep the story visually rich while moving forward, with only the minimum of dialogue and number of scenes necessary to allow us to envision the larger story.

However, we generally are working with projects where the images and scenes exist prior to the script, as in the family album. So the natural approach is to make a visual narrative, to line up the photos on a table, and then figure out what to say about the pictures. The advantage is that you can be very specific about what information you must fill in to make sense of the narrative. The dis-advantage is that if there is too big of a gap for the audience to close between images, you are left with holes in your story that you have to invent pictures to fill. We have decided that there is no right or wrong way to compose in this sit-uation—script first or image sequence first. Different people have intuitive skills in the visual or text modes.

As we consider creating material for our projects, it is also worth discussing the concept of explicit versus implicit illustration.   This takes us into the territory of metaphor and symbolism.

Invariably some part of your story calls out for the use of an image that is not literally related to the subject being described. In talking about end of a romance, you may not have an image that can literally represent loss, but you could have a photograph tearing apart, or a heart splitting into two halves. The implicit meaning, the metaphor, is clear to almost anyone.

Similarly, we can "read" the juxtaposition of visual images as having implicit meaning that is beyond what one or the other image explicitly means by itself. If we have an image of a couple sitting together, followed by the image one of the couple sitting alone next to an empty chair, we will read the juxtaposition as loss.

By considering illustrations with meaning that implicitly relate to our narra-tion, we can also solve a number of problems we have in filling in the "gaps" in our storyboard.

7. Pacing

Often the most transparent feature of a story is how it is paced. Pacing is considered by many to be the true secret of successful storytelling. The rhythm of a story determines much of what sustains an audience's interest. A fast-paced movie with many quick edits and upbeat music can suggest urgency, action, nervousness, exasperation, and excitement. Conversely, a slow pace will suggest contemplation, romanticism, relaxation, or simple pleasures.

Changing pace, even in a short digital story, is very effective. Our narrative can have starts and stops, pauses, and quickly spurted phrases. You can always change music tempo to build a sense of action or release. Moving from a panning effect on a still image that slowly stretches out our concentration, followed by a burst of images in staccato succession, staggers our senses and vitalizes the media piece.

And vitality is the essential issue. Good stories breathe. They move along generally at an even pace, but once in a while they stop. They take a deep breath and proceed. Or if the story calls for it they walk a little faster, and faster until they are running, but sooner or later they have to run out of breath and stop and wheeze at the side of the road. Anything that feels like a mechanical rhythm, anything that does not allow for that pause, to let us consider what the story has revealed, soon loses our interest.

Again, trust your own sense of what works. Everyone moves at his or her own pace.

Finally

Experience has shown us that even people with years of training in various kinds of storytelling and communication lose touch with the fundamentals of story structure and media design. These ideas are a starting point. From there you can do as we have done: develop mentors, develop a library of resources, and deepen your practice to improve your skills and develop the level of mastery that makes sense for your occupation and interests.

6 Storyboarding

What is a storyboard?

It is a place to plan out a visual story in two dimensions. The first dimension is time: what happens first, next, and last. The second is interaction: how does the audio information—the voice-over narrative of your story and music—interact with the images or video. In addition, it can be a notation of where and how visual effects such as transitions, animations, or compositional organization of the screen will be used.

Storyboarding in the film world is a high art; mixing a sense of seeing the composition of a scene to unfold before the camera, with all of the many choices available to a director regarding camera placement, focal point, duration of shot, possible edits, and camera based effects such as panning and zooming. Storyboard artists combine illustration skills, a sense of stage business (where actors, props and sets are placed before the window of the camera) with cinematography and cinematic theory to write the road map for the director and film crew to organize every part of a film production.

The art of film storyboarding has taught anyone working on a film, animation, motion graphics, web design, or digital storytelling, a singular important lesson. Planning on paper will save an enormous expense of time, energy and money when it comes time to produce your work. Taking the time to organize your script in the context of a storyboard tells you what you need to illustrate your story. If this exists, from the selection of images you have in your archive, then it just tells you the order of things and makes your edit go quickly. But much more importantly, especially with our novice storytellers, storyboards clarify what you do **not** need, and saves you from scanning, photographing, shooting video, designing in Photoshop, or recording things that simply have no place in this particular story.

Recipes for Disaster

Our cautionary tale concerns Rick, just an average guy, getting ready to make his first digital story.

"What a great morning," thought Rick, stepping out his back door and going to the little studio he had cleared out of a corner of his garage. "Today, I become a filmmaker. I am going to make my first digital story this weekend. Today, I'll assemble all the material I need. Tomorrow, I'll edit it all together."

Rick's story was a tribute to his parents. Their 40th wedding anniversary was in a week, and he had a great idea about a retrospective on their lives. He had taken the two large boxes of photos and a few old 8 mm films from his parent's home, a three-hour plane trip away. He was confident that if he could just sort through the stuff, the story would write itself. "I know that's how Ken Burns does it, just gather all the sources and piece it together like a puzzle."

He had his computer fired up. He had a scanner and digital camera handy, and the video camera set up on a tripod next to the old 8mm projector. He was going to record the film being projected against a sheet he had hung on the wall. "Ingenious," he thought to himself.

The day began smoothly. Rick organized the photos into piles representing five decades of his parent's life together. "Man, these are great, I think I'll scan these 8 from the fifties, and these 12 from the sixties, but the ones from the seventies, when I was born, god, there are at least 30 of these I have got to use." And on it went. The piles grew. No scanning yet. He broke for lunch.

Then came the film. "Old 8mm film is really beautiful, isn't it?" he thought. "My parents are going to love this part when I had my first little swimming pool. Wow. I'll just transfer it all, and then make my selections tomorrow, during the edit." A few glitches in the camera, but eventually he got it right and about 4 pm the video was recorded on the camera. He thought about taking notes about which sections were on his two-hour tape, but he was having so much fun reminiscing he never got around to it.

"Music, yeh, I have to find the right music, old show tunes and stuff. And I need a few archival images, I bet I can find that stuff on the Internet." After dinner he got online, and around 11 pm he found his eyes had become blurry and his mouse hand had gone numb. But he had the stuff—all in one big folder on the computer.

He woke up in the middle of the night. Rick opened his eyes, "You know the part where they are looking out over the Grand Canyon, I can cut to a shot of me digging myself into the sandbox when I was three. That will be soooooo cool. I can't wait to start."

The next day, he scanned, he played with Photoshop, he captured way too much video on his computer so he ran out of hard drive space. He played with his morphing software. He did everything but start on the story. Sunday evening came and it was still a big mess.

The week was a nightmare at work, so he only had a few hours to actually edit. The event approached on Saturday, and the best he could complete was an extended music video, 14 minutes long, with whole sections of images, film and titles bumping, flipping, and gyrating for reasons unknown. Several of his parent's friends fell asleep during the showing, and at the end there was a spattering of applause. Rick attributed the reaction to the heaviness of the gravy on the Chicken Stroganoff that was served at the dinner.

His mother, of course, cried through the whole thing.

His father, always supportive, thanked him, and said, "Rick, that was, well, really … interesting."

Digital stories have the advantage over film production that you are often using available material at the core of your project, but as our story shows, the material itself is profoundly compelling, particularly if it is a first visit in a long time. Without a script, and an idea of how the story is told, it can overwhelm the best of us.

Rick's tale is the worst case scenario for the digital storyteller. So much wonderful content, so many cool tools to play with, so little real idea of what they are doing. We have met many people that had symptoms of these obsessions, and in our workshop we work to try and gently bring them back down to earth. We affirm that the material is irresistible, but we encourage that first draft be written, and at least a bit of storyboard work considered, prior to diving into the archive.

Just as the professional uses the storyboard as a critical production management tool, saving countless hours of experimentation, avoiding over production of non-essential material, and wasteful over-scheduling of manpower, we want to encourage our participants to reach for their highest level of organization to maximize the precious time they have to create these movies. For many of our workshop participants, life may give them only a few such opportunities to really mine the archive for the critical stories of their lives. And frankly, their bosses, or just the demands of their lives, may give them very little time to do the projects at all.

We want to honor all different kinds of creative processes. For some, time is not so extravagant a luxury. If you can afford to excavate your archive completely, to fully examine the creative palette of multimedia tools, and to work through a series of drafts of your project to move a highly polished piece, the rewards are worth the effort.

Making a Storyboard

Our reference here is from a tutorial developed by the staff of the Center for Digital Storytelling in 1999 called *MomnotMom*, based on a reflection by staff member Thenmozhi Soundararajan. This section of the movie consists of a title and six photographs and a short video clip. The soundtrack is a nice piece of guitar music. We've laid out the storyboard on the following page.

Notice how few words of the voice-over are under each picture. Each line takes about six to 10 seconds to speak. In general, three to four seconds is about the ideal length for any still image to appear on the screen. Too short, and it's hard for the viewer to recognize what's being shown; too long, and boredom sets in. If you're laying out your storyboard and find lines and lines of text under any one picture, rethink your script or your images.

Images				
Effects	Fade In	Image Pan	Image Pan	Image Pan	Image Pan
Transitions	Cross Dissolve				
Voiceover	There is a picture of my mother that I always keep with me.		It is a curious photo, because in most photos I always imagine that people pose for the future, but in this time, this moment, this photograph, I feel like she is searching for her past.		
Soundtrack	Fade in guitar chord progression				

Images				
Effects	Alpha Channel Motion				
Transitions	Cross Dissolve	Cross Dissolve	Cross Dissolve	Cross Dissolve	Cross Dissolve
Voiceover	Across oceans and between cultures, I think back to who she was as a girl,	a young woman,	a doctor,	a wife,	
Soundtrack	guitar chord progression				

Can the script be cut down and the image left to speak the missing words? If the text remains long, can more than one image illustrate the essential words? You may also want to use some effects to extend the viewer's interest in a single still image. But for now, try to use the best effect of all: letting images speak for themselves, and using words to say the rest.

Some Ways to Make Your Storyboard

1. Get a piece of posterboard, preferably large (22" x 17"), and a packet of Post-it® notes. Sort out the image material you plan to use and label each of the Post-it notes with the name and, if needed, a phrase describing the image.

2. Create five or six rows horizontally across your posterboard, leaving room for writing text below each Post-it. Fill in the text of your script in pencil, and place the appropriate images above the appropriate words. The Post-its will allow you to move things around or take them out as need be, and you can erase the text if you want to move it around.

3. Instead of labeling Post-its with the name of each image, you could go to a copy place and photocopy your photos. (Shrink them a bit.) Tape or glue your copied images to the Post-its, and lay out your storyboard. The advantage here is that, just as on the computer, you can easily move things around.

4. If you'd like to work on a smaller page, photocopy the blank storyboard template on the next page or visit www.storycenter.org/cookbook.html and download the file storyboardtemplate.pdf.

5. If you know desktop publishing software like Adobe's PageMaker or QuarkX-press, or how to layout tables in Microsoft Word, and you're familiar with how to scan images, you can make your storyboard right on the computer.

Any of these methods will work. Do whatever is convenient and easy for you.

A storyboard will speed your work in many ways. It can show you where your voice-over should be cut before you record, and may help you to determine if you have too many or too few images chosen before you begin scanning.

Storyboarding is a valuable tool, but it can also be fun. Get others to join you in your storyboarding process and make it a collaborative project.

Images

Effects

Transitions

Voiceover

Soundtrack

Images

Effects

Transitions

Voiceover

Soundtrack

7 Designing in Digital

Issues/Ideas about working with Digital Imaging and Video

What makes good design in a Digital Story?

This is a loaded question. If you went to a design school, you would be handed a small boatload of principles and conventions for good design. The principles would cover color theory, composition, perspective, typography, photography, cinematic theory, conventions in animation and motion graphics, and a touch of audio design to boot.

For the digital storyteller, unless you are moving toward a professional career, you can save yourself a year of fundamentals classes by using the oldest principle in design, mimic what you like.

In our workshops, we show specific pieces where the participants made choices that we like, and we felt worked in the overall impact of their story. Some issues of design are obviously integral to the seven element discussion in Chapter 5: pacing, what sorts of images to use, and the issues of sound track, for example. In this chapter, we look more closely at some design issues to expand the discussion. We will discuss two movies with illustrations to examine a number of choices that are fairly typical in the course of early attempts and digital media design.

We will not be addressing how the pieces were created. All the examples were made using a mix of Photoshop and Premiere. The video and still cameras that were used represent qualities that are available at the consumer level today. We felt that offering tutorials in this book would make it out-of-date almost as soon as the book was printed. Our tutorials in current versions of software are available in a separate spiral bound companion workbook for purchase at our website, www.storycenter.org.

Barbara French's *Redheads*

We start with a look at *Redheads*, a story from the first round of digital storytelling workshops in 1994 in our San Francisco studio. This piece was a collaboration between Barbara and her son, Center for Digital Storytelling (CDS) co-founder, Dana Atchley.

In many ways we consider this a classic digital story as it is composed of a few small clips of video, and a large number of still images. Here is the script of *Redheads* to give you a context for the story. If you want to see the movie, visit www.nextexit.com/movies/redheads.mov.

> *It might be hard for you to believe that I was once a little girl. I grew up in an old farmhouse in a small town on Lake Erie in western New York.*
>
> *There were acres of grape vineyards behind our big barn ... and, one year, a field of strawberries beside the house. Down the lane was an apple tree that had three different kinds of apples on it.*
>
> *My father went to his office at the grape juice factory every weekday and played golf on weekends. He believed in germs and we had to keep our hands clean and gargle a lot.*
>
> *My mother managed the household, cooked good plain meals (and very good desserts) and took care of her three daughters Barbara (me), Martha & Ann.*
>
> *She was a handsome woman with a Roman nose, hazel eyes, pince-nez glasses and—wonder-of-wonders—Red Hair! She called it Titian and complained when the motor vehicle office made her use auburn on her driving license.*
>
> *At the time of my birth she wrote a letter to my great aunts and signed it with my name. She wrote: "My father and I look so much alike. I'm awfully glad I haven't red hair like mother's."*
>
> *I thought her red hair was really beautiful and I loved to brush and comb it. I often wished mine were like hers.*
>
> *She died of cancer when I was seventeen. Her best friend asked the nurse to cut off her long braid, and she gave it to me. I have kept it for sixty-two years in a wooden box that says "Chocolate Shop, Los Angeles"—which is where my parents were married.*

Eventually I had three daughters and a son—none with red hair. What a disappointment!

Now I am the grandmother of six grand daughters—and two of them have red hair!

Redheads
—Barbara French, Dana Atchley, Megan Atchley

In designing the piece, Dana and Barbara had a number of choices that illustrate both common design feature sets in Photoshop and Premiere, and some good production principles of design.

Framing

As a videographer, Dana was experienced in the process of interviewing subjects and the framing of his video shots. In framing his mom in the first shot of the movie, Figure 1, he demonstrates a classic middle shot for an interview, from chest up to just above the top of her head. He then allowed for a bit more room to the right of the frame, which allowed him to place the inset of her as a child.

Figure 1.

Figure 2.

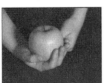
Figure 3.

In other video shots in the movie, he made careful choices about how close he would move to the shot, capturing the braid, Figure 2, and apple, Figure 3, as tight as he felt he could go.

When you are interviewing a person, whether by video, or just taking a photo, consider carefully how you frame a person. A common mistake is to take the shot too far away from the person or object.

In the video at the beginning and end, Dana almost imperceptibly pans toward his mom with the camera. In general, it is a good idea to hold your shot steady, not moving the camera or zooming in or out. If you do use zooming, use it sparingly.

Lighting

Dana shot the video with a relatively bright light above and to the right of his mom, with another bit of softer light, even with her head and to her left. He was also aware of his lighting in the other shots. In lighting design, the notion of a key light to sharpen the features, and a fill light, to fill in the shadows, is a principal convention. Sometimes this can be done with natural lighting, the light through a window, and a lamp near by. He also used richly textured or high-contrast background that helped to bring his mom and other shots out from their background. Finding a nice background, not too busy, but not just a blank wall, always makes the shot look better.

Audio

Many people have come into our workshops with videos of interviews they captured with their home video camera as part of an oral history or an experience they had. Often the audio was unusable. The most common mistake is setting up the camera across the room from someone, then zooming in on their faces to frame the shot. The standard built in microphone on a home video camera takes sound from all directions and is quite sensitive. As a result a voice gets lost in a room. The sound loss is even worse outdoors. The solution is to use either a "shotgun" microphone that create a small cone of sound that it hears in the direction the microphone is pointed, or a lavaliere microphone that you clip onto the person's shirt so that it only picks up voice.

Compositing in Video and Still Images

The first image, Figure 1, contrasts Dana's mom in her seventies, with the shot of her as a child, in the shape of a cameo we could imagine came from her youth. We are quite used to this form of inset illustration from watching the talking heads on the news each night. The convention is quite effective; you have both the dynamism of the speaker, and the graphic information of the inset.

Putting images in layers on top of each other, as in Figure 4, is referred to as compositing in the language of Photoshop and digital video editing. Composites can be as simple as a background and one image, or can be a complex collage of images stacked in interesting ways in relationship to each other. The compositing in video can also include elements

Figure 4.

like text, graphics, video within video, and animations. It is quite common to have the elements in motion as well, appearing over a series of backgrounds. The most important consideration in designing motion graphics and composited images is that the elements should service, not detract from, the story. Making a screen too busy by covering up a wonderfully compelling image with other elements may be fun as an experiment, but will detract from the story. Remember to remove your experiment before you complete your project.

Figure 5.

Figure 6.

In *Redheads*, text is used to provide information not in the script, as in Figures 5 and 6. The text is composed on the screen in a way that avoids taking away from important parts of the overall image, such as covering faces or the central focal point of the image. The composite elements move on to the screen and stay, at least for a sufficient enough period to recognize them, and usually through the end of the image being seen on the screen. They do not tend to fly-on, fly-off, and bounce around the screen.

Also note that tools like Photoshop and Premiere give you the ability to add drop shadows to the elements which may assist in them being recognizable, as in text, but also providing three dimensions to the screen by separating the foreground and background objects.

Finally, color choices for text are critical in video; warm and light colors, oranges, yellows, silvers, or whites, will work in most circumstances. Avoid blues, reds, purples and darkened colors, even if you feel they would work in print reproduction. Watching text in these colors on a monitor or television screen is difficult if not impossible.

Panning and Zooming

No tool is more associated with our style of work than the ability for a computer editing program to easily pan and zoom across an image. Panning refers to moving across the horizon of a film shot, and zooming is moving in to a point on screen, and moving in or out from the point.

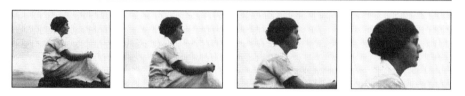

Figure 7.

Like any effect, panning should be practiced with restraint. Many first users find it irresistible and pan and zoom on every image. In *Redheads*, Dana uses the computer-generated pan only on two images, a house at the beginning, and the long pan on the profile of Barbara's mother, Figure 7. In each case, the focal point for the pan is providing an emphasis for the viewer.

We find that the use of pan and zoom is also a critical component in pacing. In *Redheads*, the edit pace is fairly dynamic until we reach the mother's profile shot. The zoom takes almost 20 seconds from beginning to end, and suddenly we are descending into the quiet heart of the emotional material. This long shot acts as a bridge between the expository material at the beginning and the context of Barbara's family in New York, and the story of the red hair. In this sense it shifts pace to focus on the information that we really need to consider in the story.

Transitions and the Blending of Imagery

Digital effects in video software almost always start with the ability to achieve a transition from one visual element to another. As such, the use of transitions is a strong tradition in a introductory digital video production workshop. The transition packages in a tool like Premiere includes 75 different transitions, from basic dissolves to peels, zooms, wipes and slides.

If you watch television and film, you will rarely see the use of transitions, almost all of the edits cut from one edit to the next. The convention for when to use transitions in film is fairly straightforward. A dissolve is used, usually to or from black, to indicate the change of time and place, as from leaving one scene and going to the next. Other effects were developed to call attention to a cool visual effect in itself, as part of the style of the film. We have seen the iris transition, a circle, star or rectangle opening or closing one scene to the next in old space-adventure serials like *Flash Gordon*, a device that George Lucas brought forward in the *Star Wars* epics.

Because we are relying on static still images, and because the style of our films can include a playful experimentation with what digital effects can show, transitions can come in handy. *Redheads* uses a number of transitions effectively, again having the choice of transition formed by the content in the images. In the beginning, there is a pan toward a

Figure 8.

garage, and as we get closer, the barn door transition opens up on a scene of the grape vineyards, Figure 8. Other wipe transitions are used that allow us, for a split second, to compare the current image with the image coming after.

Figure 9.

But by far the most common transition is the dissolve, which demonstrates the notion of blending imagery that is quite common in digital media design. In photography, the idea of double exposing a negative is fairly familiar to most of us. The effects can often be extraordinary, with the ghost of one image contrasting with another to create a more evocative collage, Figure 9. Digital media allows us to play with the relative opacity of images and video with great ease. And it allows us to experiment with various mechanisms for blending images using color relationships, relative darkness and lightness values, and hue and saturation to draw out parts of an image over another.

The fluidity of this part of the digital media palette almost defies convention, as the effective permutations are infinite. As with all effects, knowing when to stop messing with the composition, or frankly, when to leave well enough alone, are perhaps the more difficult choices for the designer.

Frank Gonzalez' *Bombast*

In 2000, we began what has become an annual workshop at the Art Center School of Design in Pasadena, California. In the first workshop a short experimental piece by Frank Gonzalez has ended up as a discussion piece for our work, because it asks the question, "Should we look back at these images and share stories with others? What right do they have to hear our intimate stories of pain and loss?" even as it provides an intimate glimpse to Frank's own story.

Here is the script. The movie can be found at www.storycenter.org/frank.

> *I bought these old photographs for a quarter each, wondering what stories they might hold. Everyone has a story they say. Me, well, I could tell you the one about my mom falling on her ass after trying to kick me when I was six. Or the one about my dad having to join the communist party in '71 in order to feed his family. Or the one about my sister dating a married man in New York City. I've had to live with these stories and I am constantly reminded of them. I don't want to make you sob or put you in a moment in my world by telling you the one of me not telling my grandpa that I loved him when I knew he was dying. My dead grandpa would be turning on his grave—how dare you tell this story.*
>
> *My memories have shaped me, made me who I am.*
>
> *I wouldn't mind living inside the photos I bought at the market. A moment in time, no precursor, no story.*
>
>
>
> *Bombast*
> *—Frank Gonzalez*
> © 2000 Frank Gonzalez. Images and Text All Rights Reserved.
>
>

Film and Montage

Figure 10.

Watching Frank's piece, you are immediately dropped into a series of loosely defined patterns—trees, underbrush, and grass (Figure 10)—that act as backgrounds for the discussion about to take place. Frank creates the sense that you are following the narrator into the woods, on a slightly surreal journey into his reflections.

Figure 11.

No sooner does he establish this sense that with his first words we see a machine gun repetition of images, Figures 11-13. Twenty-seven image frames appear, each with a different part of four separate photos on-screen for no longer than 1/10th of a second. The effect is jarring, and in the one minute 21 second piece he returns to this flashing of images six more times.

Figure 12.

At times the flash of images is no more than subliminal. The relation of the content of the images to what is being said appears as a non sequitur, providing only more of that dreamlike quality. In closer examination, the content is of course related.

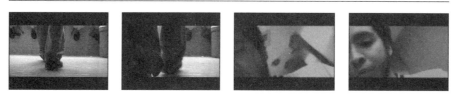

Figure 13.

Video clips were used twice in a similar, choppy image fashion, first again as part of the montage of non sequiturs, and second as a self-portrait that corresponds with the final part of the text.

Film montage works when an artist creates the conditions for the audience to absorb context, even as they excite and perhaps confuse us with visual non sequiturs. Even if there is an implicit relationship of the images that flash on or off, we cannot hope, at least on a single viewing, to create meaningful closure of their relationship. We are left with impressions, traces of the form and shape and substance of what we are seeing, that when it works, creates a dominant impression of meaning.

Frank uses both the bridge shots of tracking along the ground and the camera spinning toward a canopy of branches to establish a continuity of the author's viewpoint on the moments. At least suppose that he is considering this narrative about personal images and his own life. He tells us that some of the images that are flashing are photos he found at a store. We view his use of non sequitur and montage as part of the general unsettled tone of his writing.

The implications of montage for us non-art students are critical. When we write our stories, our first impulse is to provide the literal or explicit imagery that corresponds to what is being said. As in *Redheads*, when you hear "house by the lake," you see a house by the lake, when you hear "apple trees," you see an apple, etc. But we, and our sophisticated media saturated audiences, are quite familiar with film montage, because it is used in television advertising and music videos extensively.

Since our writing often doesn't correspond to a large number of our images, the notion of finding bridge material, images or video that provides a continuity of appropriate context but does not necessarily correspond to the story being told, can be a life saver.

Audio Design

Frank creates a dominant impression with his sound design as well. He succeeds in his choices of effect, a scratchy end-of-record on a turntable sound that sounds like crunching leaves, and the appropriate stark and foreboding ambient music, as well as his offhand and familiar performance of the script.

Most digital storytellers will not have the time for extravagant audio design, so the note here is again about restraint as much as effect. Sound effects can call attention to themselves in a big way, and they can break the rhythm in a work. Using an effect like a piece of music, a motif of barely audible laughter, or a soundbed of a low engine hum, on the level of almost imperceptible noise, will evoke their own subconscious responses. How they mix with music used, and the voice, is really the decision. When you are unclear, erring on the side of leaving it out is usually the best choice.

Experimentation— Necessity as the Mother of Invention

The other design issue to discuss about Frank's film is the role of the experimental process. Frank chooses a story, a tone poem really, that can be illustrated with almost anything, any set of images. As an experimenter, Frank searched for both a subject and method that allowed him to reach success in the shortest amount of time. Frank was like many of our students, he settled into the class slowly, and toward the end of the second day of the three-day process, switched gears and direction completely. Forget about storyboards and long research and planning processes—knock out the script and gather material as fast as humanly possible.

The images, as he suggests, are a random series of 1950's family shots and some contemporary artifacts that he could have easily had around him. All of the video is shot in and around the Pasadena campus. He has a few image effects, a blur filter here, and the colorization of his portrait video, but these aspects are quite limited. Nonetheless, his assemblage of the images in the edit happened quite quickly because he saw the edit in his mind's eye.

Final Note

We have seen a great deal of creative brilliance in the face of the unwavering deadline of our workshops. This is one of the advantages of our compressing this work into a few days. It is like using 4 x 6 cards as a writing tablet, it forces us to strip away non-essential elements. We have found, in our process, as well as in considering the processes of professional artists, that often what is finished, polished and refined becomes over-polished and over-refined and lacks the directness and spontaneity of the initial drafts.

Intuition is the largest part of experimentation. If most of our students stopped right after they completed their script, and just meditated on the message of their work, not just the order of words and their meaning, but the story's interrelationship to their entire way of looking at the world, and then went for a walk with a camera or video camera, they could successfully create an effective film just from the elements that would appear before them.

Perhaps this way of looking at digital storytelling is a bit too Zen, but it corresponds with our experience.

Interlude Three

From a Quiet Place

In 1913 my grandparents took a hunting trip in the Ozarks, shooting ground squirrels in blissful ignorance of the political turmoil in Europe. Within a year World War I would begin and my grandmother would give birth to the first of three daughters. She would outlive all of them. She survived these tragedies remarkably well with a vibrant imagination, a fondness for nonsense, and a total lack of self pity, admitting to grief but never to despair until her death at the age of 94. She had been born just days before the Battle of Wounded Knee.

My grandmother's father was a wallpaper importer in St. Louis, Missouri, a handsome man distinguished by his love of practical jokes. His fortunes changed when the second of his warehouses, uninsured, burned to the ground, a tornado destroyed their home, and he fell under a streetcar, losing a leg. A strain of creative depression runs through the maternal side of my family, claiming the lives of some of its members, but never spoken of in polite company.

My father was the youngest and only son in a family of five daughters. His father was a baker who left Germany before the outbreak of World War I to avoid the draft. None of the men in my family ever wore a uniform. They avoided conscription through intellect, draft dodging, luck and conscientious objection.

Only one of my father's sisters married. Another, whose name I do not know, died young. When asked about her, my paternal grand-

mother would only remark, "She was a Gypsy." The genetics of this family were marred by strains of intellectual brilliance and Down's Syndrome, and a poorly developed sense of humor.

I am not the progeny of long suffering immigrants, nor of an oppressed race, a victim of neither holocaust nor war. My legacy is the flower of American innocence. I have inherited the photographic records of these families, and their genetic code, but little else. Few stories accompany these snapshots of moments in time, and like victims of war, or slavery or genocide, I am forced to piece together a puzzle where are all the pieces are scattered across a continent and all historians are dead.

Nor do I have children to pass the puzzle on to. I am, to all intents and purposes, extinct.

Evolution
—Ann Jaeger

Among the clichés that inform our story mining is the one about, "still waters run deep." We have developed a tendency to look for the quiet one; the person who has only a few words to say in the story circle, who soldiers through the process disturbing the facilitators as little as possible; the one you have no real idea what they will show, or how their final script turned out.

My favorite story about this sort of experience was in the 1998 Digital Storytelling Festival and a workshop we had with 12 students up in the meeting hall of Elk Avenue in Crested Butte. The retreat nature of these "boot camps" meant a great deal of camaraderie was developed, people eating and drinking informally together, and sharing ideas and collaborating. Ann was shy about these encounters, and Nina and I checked in once in awhile, but she seemed both technically and artistically self-determined. The other students were probably screaming for help as well, and it was the usual circus of craziness on the last day.

I remember we had the computers aligned in a horseshoe. When the time came to show the work, we followed the horseshoe around to the far end of the circle, where Ann was sitting. With each piece, there were the usual cheers and applause and good-natured ribbing.

When Ann's piece played, there was a silence, one, two, three moments, and then a whoosh of exhalation as everyone shook their head, and then applauded. "Amazing" I remember saying.

I don't think this is a perfect piece of writing, although the design is visually powerful and reflects her pre-existing talents, and there is a haunting use of music. But its message, what it says about the author, and most importantly, what it says about American culture, is stunning.

I have a rap, a lecture, I share with people about how consumer culture affects story. I talk about the re-organization of people into their little pseudo-castles of security. I address how a fluid, mobile international workforce caused the rupture of community, from San Bernadino to Sao Paulo, Bonn to Benin. I always think of this story, because it captures this sense of profound alienation.

Ann has captured the dilemma. Free to make ourselves as individuals, we have evolved out of rooted memory. We, for all intents and purposes, are extinct.

Or are we? Stories like *Evolution*, as dark as they may seem, illuminate our options.

8 Digital Storytelling and the Public Speaker

Professional public speakers desire the intimacy, directness, dramatic tension, and transformational power of the storyteller. They want to move beyond the teleprompter, beyond the PowerPoint presentation, to a rich and endlessly flexible presentation environment. They also want a natural performance style—unassuming, conversational, and with as transparent a relationship to the technologies as possible.

In our work in digital storytelling, and in particular the experience of developing Dana Atchley's *Next Exit*, we addressed a number of these concerns. When Dana and I were rehearsing *Next Exit* in San Francisco, one of the first issues we had to tackle was Dana's particular performance style. Dana was not trained as a theatrical performer. He didn't act. He told stories.

Dana's awareness that he could not sustain character shaped the way *Next Exit* was constructed. Dana's roots were in the singer/storyteller tradition made popular in the folk music revival of the sixties. *Next Exit* was constructed as a flexible playlist, each digital story functioning like a song. Between each story, Dana could intersperse a conversational storytelling style. Dana had 60 possible stories that he performed in any given show. The playlist was not entirely flexible: the show had the convention of a beginning story, bridge stories to the major themes or divisions of the show, and an ending story. This was to ensure that a dramatic arc was carried throughout the show.

Next Exit's computer interface also served as a transparent prompting device. By ordering his icons and then referring to and interacting with the events on the screen, he gained additional freedom to improvise and interact with the audience without losing his place in the show.

Photograph by Jasper Johal

Dana Atchley performs *Next Exit* at the American Film Institute in February 1993.

It is easy to see how this approach to storytelling relates directly to the multimedia use in public speaking. Professionals who find themselves in public speaking capacities are not usually naturally gifted or trained actors. Acting is antithetical to their purpose. Their audiences want an authentic dialogue, not a performance.

In addition, most public speakers don't have the necessary time to memorize and rehearse their material, so they are forced to use prompting devices such as scripts, teleprompters, or the bullet points of the PowerPoint presentation. To the degree to which they are directly relying on any of these devices, they appear wooden, distant, and inauthentic to their audience. Using multimedia interfaces with icons to trigger bite-sized story elements is an obvious solution.

For the remainder of this chapter we will address in greater detail the issues of constructing a performance style similar to the one that formed *Next Exit*.

The Art of Storytelling:
The Importance of Dialogue

Theater, public speaking, and storytelling all have in common the elements of stagecraft. When we speak in front of people, we provide a number of layers of meaning beyond the text, through gesture, movement, tone, and language. Physical presence and speaking voice are a critical part of a successful performance. While these crafts can be honed to a high professional level, most of us learn essential parts of these skills from casual conversation and from watching other speakers or performers.

Theater, public speaking, and storytelling also share a rhetorical construction that reflects our awareness of the way oral transmission works with our memory. We have developed spoken word rhetorical styles of repetition, cadence, and cyclical design of the story to improve the audience's ability to remember and draw the appropriate meaning or message from the presentation.

But this is where similarity stops. Our choice in describing our work as "digital storytelling" has resonance beyond its humanist and folksy connotations. Storytelling, as defined by those who are its preservationists and practitioners, stands apart from theater and public speaking because it presumes a specific attention to the audience's role in shaping the performance.

> *"A key element of successful storytelling is dialogic. An audience at a storytelling event—as opposed to those listening to a prepared speech or play—justly expect their presence to help create a singular occasion. The story is not the same story it was when the storyteller practiced it before the concert began... A storyteller needs to acknowledge and adjust to, with some immediacy, the audience's responses, which provide a fresh and limitless source of energy, making each telling of the story a unique event."*
>
> —Carol Birch, Who Says, 1996

Actors and public speakers would argue equally that their awareness of audience alters each performance in perceptible ways. But we are not only talking about adjusting a performance to enliven the audience or hamming up a joke for a particularly receptive audience. These are almost natural exchanges that the skilled speaker or theatrical performer develops over time. What Carol Birch and her storytelling colleagues are suggesting is that a skilled storyteller makes a total assessment of the audience and the specific environment at the moment of performance, and applies a conscious restructuring of the independent elements of the story to best suit the environment.

This sounds like a tall order, but it is more or less what we do in conversation. I arrive at a party. I have a group of stories in the back of my mind at any point, some current and topical, some old and situational, and as I bump into different people, in different situations, I adjust my stories. From the brief encounter, to the cross-table exchange, to the long and intimate discussion, I might tell the same story but adjust it unconsciously in length, emphasis, tone, and language. Our success at entertaining our friends and acquaintances is equally dependent on our listening and assessing our audience, as well as the degree to which we have mastered, memorized, and practiced the story segments we are prepared to recite.

The extension of this larger idea of storytelling as a dialogic and interactive process—rather than an instructive and linear process—to a new art of digital storytelling makes sense. What is most exciting about the function of randomly accessible, nonlinear multimedia data is that, in a funny way, it returns us to the nonlinearity, the interactivity, that is the fundamentally organic way we have historically shared story with one another.

I can imagine a large number of my friends who perform as solo actors, professional storytellers, and public speakers reading the argument above and shouting, "Joe, what the heck are you talking about? People want to sit back and hear a well-told story from beginning to end, be swept up in my world. While I am sure I would be sensitive to how they are responding, I think the audience usually wants to be passive participants. If they want a conversation, they can come to a post-performance question-and-answer period."

And of course, the answer is, yes, audiences like to be swept up in story, in a novel, movie, theatrical presentation, or speech. But audiences are changing in two significant ways. First, as countless experts have noted, our attention span is getting shorter. We are a culture of channel surfers. The nascent popularity of stand-up comedy, improv, and episodic character-piece solo theater all direct anyone who is presenting on stage to examine why bite-sized narratives are particularly effective with today's audiences.

Secondly, as we move toward an interactive communications culture, we have an increased expectation that our communicators will provide the option of interaction. Broadcast media has responded to this expectation with the audience participatory talk show and, now, with Web sites and interactive games that invite interaction within the worlds or with the characters presented in the stories. In the live presentation environment, sensitivity to how you use your stories to engage participation, to provoke the sharing of other people's stories, either in real time, or as a follow-up process to the presentation, is increasingly desired, if not expected. *Next Exit*'s most repeated praise was how the show invited the audience to feel that they too had a story to tell.

Digital Spectacle versus Digital Storytelling

In discussing storytelling as the metaphor for interactive presentation, we are also staking out a territory in direct contrast to the dominant use of multimedia in both theatrical and presentational contexts: the spectacle.

We all love spectacle—the absorption of ourselves into what appears to be powers or forces that seem greater than the normative daily activity humbles us and places us in a state of awe. We like that feeling. Spectacle theater and circus has worked for 2,500 years, spectacle religion has worked for more than 1,500 years, and spectacular musical events and opera for 400 years. We've had 100 years of film, perhaps the most spectacular of all the media to date. Spectacle creates total sensory immersion, and in that state we are fairly pliant observers. Following in this tradition, multimedia in presentational environments often leans heavily on spectacular events, loud pulsating music, lots of projections, fast-moving edits, and flashing lights.

Spectacle is a low form of dramatic engagement. There are many instances when it's useful in shaping broad-brush messages that have singular meanings. However, public speakers usually have a more nuanced and complex intention for their messages. In our experience, the spectacular use of multimedia damages or obscures the message that the presenter was trying to put across.

Spectacle skews expectations. The more we flash lights and turn up the music, the more the audience expects the arrival of a messenger of God to deliver divine wisdom. Unfortunately, most of us have to admit we are not bringing messages from the Burning Bush. As a participant in a few trade shows, I cannot understand why people continue to spend enormous amounts of money on spectacular events. Most of the time, the spectacle only amplifies a thousandfold the paucity of content, leaving me squiggling in my seat in uncomfortable embarrassment for the presenter. A down-to-earth storytelling persona, especially when coupled with a seemingly transparent use of media, sets up the opposite effect.

The Digital Prop

Isn't projected and amplified media inherently spectacular? Doesn't it automatically take away from the centrality of the singular storyteller on the stage?

This is a critical question. The art of storytelling often assumes the lack of device, nothing between you and your audience but your voice and your physical being. One way storytellers further distinguish between themselves and theatrical artists is that they have a reduced concern for scenery, lighting, atmospheric music or sound effects that assist in creating mood in the stage production. The magic of storytellers is that they create all the effects from the incantations of their voices, words, and physical expression.

Storytellers have also always had a tradition of using props—a rope, an image, a mandala, or other device—as visual and mnemonic devices. Multimedia in a storytelling or presentation context should assume the same role. It should be a digital prop.

What kinds of props are multimedia assets? When I was studying theater in college, my mentor Travis Bogard told me that there were three things with which actors should avoid sharing the stage: dogs, children, and fire. Multimedia falls into the fire category. If a storyteller lights a fire on stage, you watch the fire. Large projections of text, high-resolution images, and video simply outperform the performer in terms of the visceral attraction to our retina.

So it is true, we are dealing with a very powerful prop. It can become an effective aide or a distracting nuisance. How do we keep the role of the performer at the center of the presentation?

In *Next Exit*, Dana Atchley did two things to guarantee that the focus of the performance remained on him and his story. First, he created a separate visual setting for his role as performer. Dana came on and lit his video campfire, a little TV sitting on a pile of wood playing a tape loop of a fire. He sat on his only other set piece, a log. When possible, he supplemented this with a spotlight on this specific scene. Dana was not immersed in the backdrop of his projection; he was in a separate space. His relationship to the screen was external, he pointed to it, he responded to it, but he was not "in" it.

Secondly, he used a wireless mouse to control the events on the screen via the projected interface that drove his show. This added another degree of focus on the performer. While Dana's videos and images were extraordinarily compelling, he could stop them at any point, reassert his presence, and focus on his conversation with the audience. The media was his prop; he played with it as it suited any given performance. The fact that he rarely chose to interrupt the flow of his performance by starting and stopping is not the point. It is the evidence of his control of the media that sustained his centrality on stage.

The Computer as a Character

One step up from the performer's relationship to the computer as a flexible prop is introducing the computer's role as a character in the performance. Our friend Mark Petrakis, another collaborator at the Institute for the Future, has suggested that true digital storytelling will not begin until we have well-designed interactive agents that will allow us to create a dramatic dialogue with our computers, on the stage and in our everyday life.

We are all familiar with the prompting agents in a computer interface that pop up and direct action. It is not a big stretch to imagine increasingly complex use of characterizations to expand a storyteller's options in adding comic relief and dramatic tension to the tale.

Facing the Demons

> *"Stage fright has been labeled the number one fear in America by a number of different books, including The Book of Lists. It ranks higher than the fear of war, disease, or snakes. Most people are more afraid of speaking in public than they are of death."*
>
> *From Bill Mooney and David Holt. The Storyteller's Guide.*

When I read that quote I thought a great deal about who might be reading this book. And I thought about my work with Dana over the past ten years and our work as teachers of digital storytelling. When it comes down to it, we are trying to use the computing machine to address a fundamental conflict in the deepest recesses of most of our souls. We all want to be heard, but most of us feel extremely ill at ease putting ourselves in a public position to be heard.

The vast literature of psychological and artistic self-help guides to storytelling and public speaking all spend a considerable time discussing ways to overcome stage fright. Besides the need to master your material, the emphasis of most of these guides is on your relationship to your audience. You should realize your audience is pulling for you. You should find a way to carry on a conversation with the audience, even if it means choosing a few friendly people to act as your conversational partners.

Performing is about skill, but it is also about natural charisma. Charisma is a quality that all of us have to a greater or lesser degree. Having worked with so many wonderful, creative people, I have come to believe *charisma is a function of a profound sense of empathy.*

What many of the finest artists, both professional and amateur, share is a particular psychological approach to recovering from crisis. Many people who pursue an artistic path share the experience as a child of the death of a close family member or friend, their own near-death experience, or an equally intense event. Their recovery from that event left them with a particular sensitivity to the suffering of others. For some, that sensitivity becomes an unconscious drive to enact suffering and recovery again and again in a public setting, which is at the heart of the dramatic experience.

By understanding that the idea of connecting with our own vulnerability, by expressing our return from the abyss of a personal crisis, by stating our fear, we invariably connect with our audience. We also invariably understand some of the reasons we are afraid to speak on stage in the first place.

9 The Story Circle

Process and Participation in the Digital Storytelling Workshop

Beginning with this chapter through the end of the book, we will be addressing the issues of facilitating a Digital Storytelling Workshop. Many of our workshops are aimed at encouraging educators and training professionals to adapt our methods to their particular practices. We approach our work as grassroots artists, and what we describe as methods, are no more than practical values and principles that inform our practice. In sharing our experience, we hope to encourage a dialogue with our peers and the participants of our workshops about how we can continually expand and improve our efforts.

Going There

In 2000–2001, over a twelve-month period, I mourned the passing of three of the most important people in my life. I eulogized them, stood witness with the community of their friends about how much they had given the world, and sent their bodies to turn to ash. I spent most of my days going through the mechanics that the activities of my work and personal life required, but at least half of me was walking around in a constant internal dialogue with the dead, far away from this place, this world.

In June of 2001, I returned from organizing the memorial for my mother, Latane Lambert, in Austin, Texas to a busy schedule. As we have each summer, a long line of workshops awaited me, stretching from the end of June through mid-September.

The first of these workshops was a group of teachers who had been assembled as part of year-long Fellowship program run by the Interactive University at Berkeley, California. They were a tremendous assembly from Oakland, Berkeley and San Francisco public schools. They were warriors all, and I was truly humbled at their commitment and endurance. We had a relatively luxurious seven days to work with them, thinking, writing, reflecting and developing their digital stories.

As we approached this workshop, working with Francesca Saveri, a colleague of ours working on professional development and support in the Oakland schools, we developed a number of writing exercises to have them look both at the long view of their professional careers, the big values and motivations that led them and sustained them in their profession, and also the issues of the last year in their classroom. We not only wanted them to tell us what they knew was going right; but also, for them, in the safety of this circle of colleagues, to tell us about the days where they felt failure and frustration. We were far enough away from their schools, and the school year, that this sort of perspective was possible. Our goal was to have these writing prompts lead them to stories that would stand as assessments of their practice. The fellowship would give them a year of dialogue with each other and the ability to return to tell another story informed, we hoped, by the perspectives the year of work would provide.

On the first morning, as we often do, we introduced everyone to each other, presented the overview to our work, background, and a number of digital stories that illustrate various aspects of application and design success. We completed this showing just before lunch, and several of the participants asked me if I had created any stories. Of course, I had, and the one that particularly called to me was the memorial piece for my brother from the year before. I didn't really stop to think about it. I just went to my office, found the file, and put it up on the projector.

What I hadn't thought about was how this might hit me at that moment. I crumbled. I fell to the floor. As close to a full sobbing release of emotions as I have experienced. Here, in front of a group of relative strangers, as the teacher, as the person in charge, I had lost it. Completely.

And you know what? It was as natural as rain.

The workshop went really well.

Sacred Time, Circles of Story

We do not pretend, at the Center for Digital Storytelling, to have license to function as a therapeutic encounter. The material that explains and markets our work does not suggest that this environment should be formally approached as a healing process.

But it would be inconceivable, incomprehensible, and downright irresponsible, if we did not recognize the emotional and spiritual consequence of this work.

As we told in the story of our initiation into this work, the forbearers of traditions of the story circle are indeed ancient, they source back to root traditions in every one of our cultures. They of course remain vital in the root cultures that survive to this day, most certainly in the living traditions of our Native peoples and their ceremony.

What we know is that when you gather people in a room, and listen, deeply listen to what they are saying, and by example alone encourage others to listen, magic happens.

The magic is simple.

We do not have many safe places to be heard.

Storytelling, sharing personal reflective storytelling in a group is a privilege. In our cultures, those of us who live fully in the modern world of commutes, deadlines, distractions, and endless objects and activities of our desires dancing before our eyes; do not go easily into quietude and listening. We mainly talk at each other, not to each other.

The result is the stressful sickness of modern living.

Cherishing Story

When we organize our workshops, or talk with others about initiating their own programs and workshops, we stress the responsibility of the facilitator. If the workshop process is working, and a circle of trust established, people will take risks, and their relationship to the story becomes tangibly powerful for them. The stakes for participants are serious.

Anything less than reverence for each and every story can result in a deeply emotional sense of betrayal. People put themselves into these stories in ways that totally surprise them. Usually, they cannot prepare themselves for these feelings.

One manifestation of this underestimation is participants not taking the procedures of securing and backing up their project of their own accord. As such, our center has made it a matter of principle that every project, every file associated with the project, and every movie is archived, with a copy made for the author, and a copy in our own archive as a back-up.

We have only lost a story once in the last five years. In the summer of 2000, we had a two teachers come from Detroit to our workshop in Berkeley to collaborate on their project. Their material was somehow lost.

We flew a staff member to Detroit to re-work and re-edit the project.

Looking at the Workshop Process

Like any classroom or group process, each workshop is unique. Each facilitator has a unique approach to their work that shapes the tone and feeling of workshops. However, we have drawn some overall lessons about the various steps in the process that assist us in the attempt to sustain a consistent attitude of nurturing and solemnity.

The typical digital storytelling workshop is three days. On the first day we have an introduction process, an overview to digital storytelling, a script review and development session, and usually a tutorial in Photoshop. The second day begins with an introduction to the video editing software (Premiere or other), and then we move to a full production phase of the work which carries us through Day Three. In some workshops, we divide the Video Editing Tutorial between demonstrating how to complete a basic edit on one day, and all the special effects features on the morning of the final day. The workshops end with a showing of the work.

To produce a digital movie, the production process involves four distinct steps.

1. **Importing material to the computer.** This involve scanning and digitizing audio and video either prior to or during the workshop. Recording the voice-over is a critical part of this process, and we usually insist on this being done in our lab in order to sustain quality.

2. **Preparing material for use in your movie**. In our situation, this is principally a process of some Photoshop work to adjust, manipulate, size and design images. In a professional environment this might include pre-producing the audio and some specific video work to enhance the quality of the original footage.

3. **The initial video edit or rough edit**. We encourage participants to complete a rough cut of the movie, without transitions or special effects. The rough cut allows the participant to have an overview to their project, as well as identifies the areas where materials, images or video, are insufficient for the edit.

4. **Special Effects, Creating Titles, Audio Mix**. The final run through the project is to look at ways to enhance the project by using any of the hundreds of filters, transitions, motion graphics, compositing, audio layers and mix, and text generation available on many of the digital video editing tools. This is why digital video editing is fun, but is also where novices can become overwhelmed, or just get lost in attempting to sort out all of the possibilities. We emphasize a specific set of tools that orients the novice to start simple and expand their creativity over time with the tool.

Project duration is also an important parameter for the success of the workshop. We suggest in all our materials that the goal is a three to five minute movie. In some cases, where we know the technical situation is complex, or the amount of time for preparation is limited, we suggest 2–3 minutes. As part of setting these limitations, we suggest a script length of one to one and one-half double-spaced typewritten pages. We also suggest that the participants limit their material to 15 still images and no more than two minutes of video selections.

As often as not, participants arrive with a large selection of material, but only the outline of a story. Our expectations are that the participants complete the story by the first day, and record their narrative no later than the end of the second day. This leaves them at minimum one day for editing.

1. **Introductions**. At the beginning of our workshops, we make sure that introductions are comfortable and complete. We engage people who are feeling reticent about their participation, prodding for a bit more background, or joke assuringly about everyone's shared fear and uncertainty in participation. At the same time, we carefully gauge the extent of their reticence so as not to overwhelm them and to respect self-assessed measurement of social distance in the group process.

2. **Initial Lectures**. We make our lectures as short as possible, providing, we hope, an entertaining context for their attendance, and inspiring them with ideas and examples. We assess with each and every gathering to what extent the message is sinking in, or bouncing off, because of the innumerable issues that are occupying the participants at the beginning of the workshop.

3. **Script Review**. In re-gathering for the group script review, our approach is to mix the designation of who should be asked to share their script or story ideas with encouraging volunteers. We will use the initial introductions as an assessment as well, trying to make sure we are not putting the more vulnerable on the spot. We also try to avoid having who we might assess as the "prize" student who is well-prepared and already skilled in their writing and presentation skills, go too early in the script circle, thereby intimidating everyone else.

   We attempt to demonstrate by our own presence an extremely high degree of concentration to each and every story. We generally discourage summarily any interruptions, such as people talking, or working in another part of the room. When each participant has the floor, as facilitators, we make sure we engage them with our own eye contact, as well as bring the other participants into the group process by drawing their eyes (and ears) into the conversation.

   We approach asking questions or giving feedback person by person. All of our facilitators bring to the discussion all the skills of story development, script analysis, peer counseling, mothering, love, and sheer willpower they have at their disposal. We create a group dynamic, while carefully monitoring how feedback is given, so as to avoid overwhelming the participant. We are particularly aware of the kinds of individuals that seem incapable of stopping themselves from wanting to oversee every project in the room and potentially steam roll the more reticent participants to their given vision of the interpretation of the story.

4. **Tutorials**. We have designed our tutorials in Photoshop and Premiere, and trained our facilitators in running the tutorials, with a number of important considerations as well. The tutorials follow closely the actual production process; the steps the participants will need to follow to complete the work. The tutorials are a mix of information; what is necessary, and what inspires creativity. We have found that providing just the basics, or even designing based on a template, may make our job easier, but it deadens many participants' initiative. We want their introduction to new media creativity to have a magical, almost transformative, feeling. We also want to provide a broad

enough palette of tools that participants with the usual range of experience that we find in our workshops (true novices to professionals) have an appropriate amount of toys with which to play.

The subject matter of the tutorials is chosen carefully as well. We want them to be working on content that is relevant to the kind of projects we expect them to make, with compelling and relevant imagery and inspired writing.

5. **The Production Process.** The true art of the digital storytelling workshop however is perhaps the supervision of the production process that occurs throughout the workshop. Every individual has a set of unique creative problems to solve. It can be the script, the visual components (which images, too few, too many, not compelling, not appropriate; video that needs logging and selecting), the facility with the software or the computer, the voice recording, the creative decisions in the edit, the special effects.

   If instructors are tied up assisting someone, and another person needs help, we encourage participants to assist other participants as necessary. We identify people in each group with pre-existing skills or the aptitude at the process, and place them in appropriate distance to those who may need more help.

   In the midst of these creative and production processes, there is also the maintenance and supervision of the computers themselves, unruly beasts that they are. We can assure all those who have tried to initiate a computer lab to digital storytelling that the experience for the computers reaches a battlefield hospital proportion of symptoms, cures, work-arounds, and retirements.

   In fact, the battlefield hospital is an apt metaphor for the whole procedure. Our facilitators chart progress formally through the various stages of the production work for each student. What they don't chart are the side assessments by the facilitators based on a triage approach to each student. Some participants will make it through fine with a minimum of intervention. Some students will succeed only if active and consistent intervention is applied. And finally, regrettably, we also have students for whom no amount of intervention will result in a completed project on the deadline. We negotiate with the final type of student to insure their perspective on the process is as positive as possible, and where possible design a means for their continuing work.

6. **Final Showing.** The final showing of movies is the most critical and successful part of our workshop process. As we approach the appointed hour, the participants have finally shed their anxieties and learning is usually taking

place. As we bring an end to the workshop, we stop to recognize all that has been achieved. We also assure the participants that everyone would like additional time to complete their projects, and that each and everyone has a pre-requisite disclaimer about the projects.

Before showing the films, we ask each participant to give comments about their efforts. In general, we take care to assure that the computers external audio is working and everyone can see the screen, when the movie is shown.

Many, many tears have been shed at these showings. The release for the makers, the pride, the sense of awe at what others in the room have accomplished, the general camaraderie, are the picture of satisfaction.

The circle is closed in this final process, usually with recognition by the lead facilitator of all the students work, of the efforts of the other facilitators and volunteers, and a final comment or two.

About Facilitating the Three Day Digital Storytelling Workshop

We approach the certification of our lead facilitators with an enormous degree of care, as it goes without saying that if a person attempts to implement many parts of our process without the requisite skills, large sections of the delicate infrastructure that make the workshop succeed, can collapse. The result can turn from one of the most rewarding experiences in their life, to one of the most difficult and dismaying.

Time management is a critical component of the facilitation process. Facilitators are careful about not being drawn too deeply into one project or group of projects at the sacrifice of others. As in most project-oriented classrooms, the facilitator must sustain an awareness of the general flow of each part of the process. At times, the script process may extend to several hours, at which point, the tutorials need to be adjusted in duration.

We view the approach of an intensive retreat session, where all other distractions are minimized, and where participants can lose themselves in their work, as optimal. Students learn faster, and retain more, as well as take risks and experiment. The intensive pace also services issues of file management and post-production which can become complicated when projects are sustained over weeks and months. Many of our colleagues in schools, community settings, and businesses do not have the ability to hold multi-day intensive retreat sessions. Initial workshops may lead to weekly sessions that take months to complete. What is gained is a degree more sanity to the process. What is lost in the longer forms of this process is the sense of daring, of impossibility, and the wonder, the degree of elation that is compressed into three days.

However you help others to facilitate a story, respect the process and the participant's efforts. In the end, a well managed process guarantees the best digital stories will come to life ... and perhaps, live forever.

10 Applications

Reflections of the Meaning and Uses of Digital Storytelling

In 10 years of work in digital storytelling, the applications of this practice have spanned an enormous range of possibilities. In the following chapters, we will have conversations with a group of practitioners in the context of community activism, violence prevention and public health, education, and business. As a preface, we want to touch upon a number of applications that help to illustrate the potential range of this practice in many fields. The following tale imagines just how many ways even one person might discover the role of digital storytelling.

Sally and Her Stories

Sally first heard about digital storytelling a month before from an article in a trade magazine. She was the owner of a small custom woodworking company in Roanoke, Virginia. Sally had learned most of the new media skills as part of her graduate MBA program at Virginia Tech, so she figured she could learn the software pretty quickly. She had been looking at ways to provide a bit more pizzazz for the company's field marketing, and had the idea of using the stories as part of an electronic calling card she had made for zapping onto clients' PalmPilots. They could then watch them as a follow-up to her visits.

After her second cup of coffee and disposing of the email that was backed up from the prior day, she had started working on her script. Sally's approach was a story about her father, an amateur woodworker, and her memories of his shop. She knew her own sense of quality in design and commitment to helping people would translate to the message about her company's products and services. Besides, the building trades were filled with closet geeks these days and she knew almost every contractor would dig seeing pictures of these old tools and a sawdust-filled shop. "They are all romantics about the "art" of construction," she thought to herself. She would start on the project tomorrow.

As she commuted home that evening, the talk radio program had a story about a senior center that was about a mile from her house. A group of seniors had begun an oral history project with the sixth grade class at her daughter's school working with the History Museum of Western Virginia. They were making digital stories about the period of segregation, and memories of race relations from the 1950's and before. "Hmm," she thought, "what a great idea."

When she got home, her husband was sitting at the computer. "What are you doing, honey?" she asked. "Hey," he responded, hardly taking his face from the screen, "I just started working on this little movie, a digital story, about my dad. I wanted to honor him in some way. We were talking about doing this in my grief-counseling group. Ever since he died, it just feels like I haven't ..." his words trailed off. She saw a tear falling from his eye, which surprised her, he rarely cried. She hugged him, "I think that's wonderful, what can I do to help?"

Before he could respond, the phone rang, and she decided to let the machine take it, but when she heard the excited words of her son, Malcolm, a sophomore at Howard University, she ran and grabbed it.

"Mom, you won't believe," he was clearly agitated. "What's going on, baby," Sally asked, concern in her voice. "Mom, I just got back from this big rally by the Capital, it was the Million Youth March for Justice. It was great, and I shot all this video. I am going to make story about it for the next organizing meeting of the Howard chapter. Isn't that great?!"

"Yes, yes, you do that, and send me a copy on DVD, okay?"

As she hung up, she looked at the favorite picture of her with her parents hanging on the wall by the phone. Her parents were in

dashikis from the 1970's, and she had her finest Angela Davis-revo-
lutionary-sister look. They were at a rally. It was her sophomore
year at Howard.

Swelling with pride, she shook her head and thought, "The circle's
not broken, not now, not ever."

Telling an Organization's Story

Whether you are working for a commercial enterprise or a civic group, trying to capture an organization's story is a common idea for a digital storytelling project. For some, this is just another piece of marketing material, a step up from a PowerPoint presentation, and a step below spending $20,000 on a new promotional video. For others, the style of personal narrative, in a piece that is produced with a minimal, but elegant design, stands out as a new way of communicating meaning and values in relationship to the products or services the organization offers.

Our work in telling organizational stories has gone from the smallest one-person outfits to assisting the marketing professionals working with huge corporations. As Dana Atchley described in the interview in Chapter 14, the thrust of organizational stories revolves around the question of "What Does the Organization Mean to You?" You can of course, in the advertising tradition, gather the testimonials about the people affected by your organization or consumers of its products. Those stories would be familiar. But as a person whose work life revolves around representing the organization, you should have a good answer to the question. And no matter how good you are at making up reasons for supporting the organization, if your answer does not stir emotions, does not connect with an aspect of your life's calling, then in our book, you are not likely to be that effective in any of the materials you create.

So our approach to an organization's story always starts with a person connecting their life experience to the organization's mission or branding. It may not be the story that makes it into your next speech, organizational website, or broadcast publication, but until you create it, you probably will not do as good a job of representing other people's stories for the same organization.

Reflective Practice

We recently had a student arrive, and in the first introductory circle, describe the project she was doing about her boyfriend, and that well, at the end of the movie, she wanted final words to, ah, propose to him. It was our first marriage proposal digital story, and it told us that we had crossed yet another threshold in the potential of the form.

If we were to ask the students that come to our monthly workshops in Berkeley, what brings them, the majority would undoubtedly say they have a project due tied to some important part of their life process; unique travel experience or adventure, weddings, anniversaries, birthdays, memorials, work or academic achievements. It is obvious that digital storytelling serves this need.

What is not so obvious is how digital storytelling works as a reflective practice. We have addressed how intimate our relationship is with many of our photos, and the well-established effectiveness of writing story as a form of reflection. What is a bit more complex is to describe how video editing, particularly with the addition of photographic manipulation and special effects, is in itself a powerful new set of reflective tools.

We have observed that as people not only look, speak and write about the material they have drawn from their historic archive, but manipulate, colorize, zoom in and around, re-composite and create collage out of these valued images and artifacts, that the material comes to life. This re-animation, and the plasticity of change—things can be tried, and re-tried, again and again and again—helps the participant to actually manage their meaning. In providing the play space for these manipulations, the production process becomes re-generative in itself.

We look forward to a time where cognitive scientists and therapeutic researchers look more closely at the tools of multimedia as an extension of our understanding of art and narrative therapies.

Intergenerational Connection

When we began our work at the Digital Clubhouse (www.digiclub.org) in Silicon Valley in 1996, we immediately discovered that digital storytelling was an excellent tool for intergenerational connection. Since its inception, the Clubhouse was organized around a principle of serving a diverse cross-section of the

South Bay community, seniors and youth being perhaps the highest priorities. Since that time, a large number of senior focused workshops were organized including over a half dozen World War II Memories projects. The seniors bring the stories, the youth assist with multimedia production, and the middle generation acts as the organizational glue.

Giving a platform and focus for our elders to share their lives is served tremendously by digital storytelling. The process of organizing images, preparing a script, capturing the voice and assisting with the editing process can stimulate discussions and dialogues that go way beyond the subject and issues that make it into the final film. The transmission of values from the elders to the younger generations is also invaluable.

For youth, the service model of cross-generational digital storytelling grounds the new technologies in meaning and community. Instead of viewing new technology as a playground for their generation, they come to understand the potential liberating impact it can have for all people. It also affords them the opportunity to confront frailty, aging, mortality, and disability associated with aging in an environment of mutual respect.

Digital storytelling makes an appropriate adjunct to a more traditional oral history projects. Not only are the seniors' contributions and stories honored, but so is their authorship, their creativity, and their point of view.

Disability

It was also at the Digital Clubhouse that we began work exploring the relevancy of this practice for the many differently-abled people in our communities. One of our first projects was, *My Life As A Movie*. The project was predicated on the idea that many high school age youth with disabilities faced difficult times finding appropriate part-time or full-time employment, and perhaps going through the process of creating a digital reflection on their lives, strengths and skills, could advance the job search process for them.

In the course of the workshop we met many extraordinary youth, several of whom became an integral part of the Clubhouse youth program. We also were first familiarized with the advances in assistive technology which would allow participants likes Kevin Lichtenberg, who operated the computer using a infrared mouse tracking device attached to his forehead, to design and create their stories. Giving voice takes on new meaning to those with hearing disabilities that can "see" their voice for the first time displayed as a waveform on the computer.

Since this time, we have a number of other opportunities to work with members of the disability community in developing digital story work. In particular, in our collaboration with Prof. Sue Schweik at UC Berkeley and activist/artist Neil Marcus, we developed a digital storytelling component to a class on Creative Writing and the Body. The class was aimed at having a dialogue about disability and many of the larger cultural issues that are raised by our perceptions of self and our bodies. This meant confronting issues about the notion of limitation itself, and how our story is shaped whether we are perceived to be visibly whole, visibly limited, or invisibly limited in countless ways.

The stories of struggle, the stories of resolve, the stories of frustration and beauty, were captured elegantly in the digital storytelling process. There is no question that the larger canon of literary and creative accomplishment coming from this community will be served by various adaptations of digital storytelling processes.

Youth Programs

Three months after we started the San Francisco Digital Media Center in 1994, we found ourselves working with Ron Light, a local educational media expert, to develop D*LAB. D*LAB would remain a program of our center for almost four years allowing us to sustain an active body of work with teens from throughout San Francisco's many diverse communities. As projects we explored digital video stories, as well as web-based stories, and special workshops with specific schools and the Title IX program of the San Francisco Unified School District working with Native American youth.

As our work with the Digital Clubhouse expanded in 1996–97, we also designed curriculum for the initial round of multi-week training program for the Digitally Abled Producer Program, or DAPP, and this became and remains the central youth wing of the Clubhouse work.

These experiences affirmed our attitude that young people, despite feeling adept at multimedia tools, long for environments where freedom of expression is possible, where they can choose what story, and how their story can be told. After school environments like D*LAB and the Digital Clubhouse are often where natural learning projects can best be developed. They give young people a sense of real world consequence that is a critical component of a constructive educational philosophy. And for the most part, the students or instructors, are not weighted down with the criteria of assessment and bureaucratic inertia that plagues many of our public school settings.

As also has been stated by a number of our colleagues working in the context of media literacy with youth, digital storytelling plays an ideal intermediary role between processes of observing and analyzing media (the classic media literacy curriculum), and full-on film and video production. We learn most about the way media affects us by making our own editing decisions, and manipulating media.

Youth video, animation and film projects have demonstrated that the desire to speak in the language of film is virtually universal among our youth. However, the expense in time and resources in organizing film production is still prohibitive for this to become universally accessible. Digital storytelling puts the participant in the editing chair, with the minimal amount of preparation. Young people walk away from their first video-editing experience with a new set of eyes and ears, as they see how special effects and design decisions are constructed, and work upon our minds.

With the current commitment to educational technology use in classrooms and youth programs throughout the developed world and much of developing world, we can imagine that digital storytelling and other forms of digital media publishing will become fully integrated into all aspects of curriculum and most youth center, after-school youth programs.

We believe the future of these digital storytelling youth programs will be an integration of the youth-centered story and creative experience with the kinds of service and activist oriented models such as the Digital Clubhouse and Third World Majority (see below).

Identity and Diversity

African-American historical leader W.E.B. Dubois' incandescent pronouncement, "The problem of the twentieth century is the problem of the color line," informs our work in the twenty-first century as well. Much of the discussion about "Digital Divides," "Serving those At-risk," and "Cultural Equity" are the sophisticated euphemisms for discussions of race in our culture. No cultural work, and digital storytelling is no more than another form of cultural work, can be promulgated without addressing a point of view about race.

Digital storytelling has been seen as vector for two of the more complex aspects of this discussion. First and foremost in our point of view, every culture has the right of folks to carry on conversations, form organizations, and amalgamate their own stories outside of the discourse with mainstream culture. Integration into a dominant culture that sustains many aspects of the legacies of genocide, segregation and racism in many of its institutional practices is not the end goal of a culturally plural policy. We have encouraged the development of programs to assist people within the African-American, Latino, Asian-Pacific Island and Native American communities to capture their own stories using approaches and methods that reflect both historical cultural practice and the many contemporary expressions and ideas within these communities. Our conversation with Thenmozhi Soundararajan in Chapter 11 addresses these issues in more detail.

The other aspect of a cultural democratic practice is to provide mechanisms for people who have felt excluded from the channels of economic and political access a vehicle for projecting their stories into the mainstream. We have encouraged all of our participants to imagine their stories as having broad relevancy to a larger public, and where appropriate, to seek broadcast and other venues for distribution.

As an example of a model of the first process, we were involved, through our associates China Ching and Thenmozhi Soundararajan, in a workshop with a group of Native Californian activists, the Circle of Voices project, in the Spring of 2001. As principle, the workshop was not to allow visitors or observers, and the artifacts, many of which represented sacred items to the various communities, were not to be shared with a community outside the circle of participants. As a final precaution, none of the associated digitized materials, at the end of the project, were to remain at our center, nor were the stories to be distributed or exhibited in any fashion.

In general, CDS has sought to sustain diversity in the workshops at our center. We have an ongoing scholarship and outreach effort to reach out to communities of color. When possible we have also provided technical and production support to the grassroots efforts of our colleagues working in the multi-cultural neighborhoods of the greater East Bay.

Activism

While many of the dialogues about identity and diversity reflect an activist bent, we see the implementation of digital storytelling as part of the community organizer's tool kit, as having a unique set of considerations as well.

When my father arrived in a small East Texas town to begin an organizing project at the local garment factory, his first project was the creation of an agitational newsletter. The newsletter captured the stories about what was going on in the plant, what abuses by which managers, what information about the company's plans, what funny incidents that demonstrated flashes of spontaneous resistance. He told stories, as much as possible, in the words of the folks living the experience.

In my own activist experience, while I prided myself on being able to knock out an effective rabble-rousing speech, I knew what made my arguments for change and resistance effective were the direct examples of courage and leadership that I had observed. Capturing these stories was what breathed life into our ideology.

Of course, part of the problem with political people on the left and the right is they often make sure that the stories that are projected suit their ideologies and political programs. The "politically correct" stories are the only ones that surface in their campaigns. In a long-range view, common sense suggests that the activist leave the sifting through the arguments of the range of stories to the audience, and focus on facilitating voice and educational empowerment as broadly as possible.

Your own political stance aside, imagining how digital storytelling can be easily integrated into motivational and empowerment strategies for change is not difficult. In our own work, we have had countless activists develop projects that address the issues of their work. The media has been presented as part of meetings, assemblies, rallies and in organizing packages distributed to their audiences.

In addition, using the workshop as a solidarity and team-building exercise has been shown to be effective. If the resources are available, and for social change organizers resources are always minimal, gathering a group of organizers together to share their own stories, as well as learn the process and tools set, can orient and energize a campaign.

Curriculum

Educators have been an integral part of our practice from the start. The leading proponents of new uses of educational technology for project-based learning saw digital storytelling as one of the most obvious and effective tools for the broad cross-section of curriculum. For many educators, storytelling and learning are virtually synonymous.

In language arts and social sciences, we have seen the implementation of our process directed straight toward the subject matter. Writing and voice, reflections on civic processes, oral histories, and essays on major subject areas are just some of the ways the work has been integrated into curriculum.

We imagine a much broader role for digital storytelling in an integrated constructivist learning setting that easily could address the areas of science and math as well.

We agree with the philosophy that suggests that if child remembers the stories of their own learning process, and the application of their unique set of strengths in the various intelligences they possess, they will develop their own strategy for learning. More than the facts, formulas, and data they are expected to regurgitate as evidence of their mastery of knowledge, this strategy will service not only their academic success, but their life success.

Building a portfolio of learning stories through digital storytelling, of how students approached problems individually or in collaboration, detailing the steps and actions their approaches inspired, and reflecting on the insights that their eventual success, or possibly failure, reveal; provides a vivid and enjoyable mechanism for charting the development of their learning skills. Just imagine, a student capping their career with an interactive performance work of stories that show their work on projects from kindergarten through college, projected at the graduation party.

As educators, learning not only how to facilitate digital storytelling, but how to articulate judgments about the design grammars of video, with the same authority they have with text, is still a ways in coming. Similarly, we are at least another couple of generations on the PC Windows world of computing before we can honestly say all of the production processes associated with digital storytelling are practical in a classroom. In ten years, we have no doubt that these toolsets, and the training of the educators to use and assess with them, will have found their way into every classroom in the U.S.

Scenario Planning/Futures Thinking

In 1997, we began a multi-year collaboration with the Menlo Park-based Institute for the Future (IFTF) to look at the role of digital storytelling in scenario development. IFTF has always integrated a narrative approach its reporting methodology, combining essays examining major technological trends with fictional scenarios involving characters as consumers and managers a decade or more into the future. They were also involved in looking at the ways that new media technologies could be more thoroughly integrated into knowledge management and organizational communication. As such, digital storytelling integrated easily into their own methodologies and practices. In 1998, they commissioned CDS to create a white paper on our work, of which a several articles are excerpted in this book.

Of particular interest to us were a pair of projects involving educators and high school youth (2000), and then community members (2001), where IFTF and CDS staff collaborated in extended workshops to both educate representatives of these populations in the implications of the trends being looked at in IFTF research, and to gather stories from the representatives about their views of the future and impact of technology on their lives.

In our work with educators and students we were struck by the ability of each group to imagine the impact that technological progress would have on their personal and professional lives. With the community members who were also involved in a longer assessment of their current attitude toward technology, we were impressed by the ease in which they saw integrating the commitments and values they currently hold most dear into a future and some of the enabling technologies on the horizon. In both cases, there was recognition that technological progress had a Janus-like role in their lives, enabling and oppressing, at the same time.

The stories themselves were surprisingly powerful, given that the style of speculative writing, and the notion of illustrating the future in image, was new to all participants. We found this process assisted all of the participants to think more broadly about historical change in their communities. We imagine much more elaborate programs for capturing and developing stories about how individuals imagined their futures could be an ideal process for initiating large-scale community development campaigns.

Professional Reflection

A large number of professionals have integrated in their organizational practice some form of periodic review and assessment. Management consultants in both the commercial and civic sectors have developed numerous elaborate approaches aimed at giving the organization and the individual the opportunity to take stock of their development and morale on the job. Whether in group or as one-on-one assessments with peers or supervisors, story has always been a part of these processes. As with any reflective practice, the process is usually more important than the product. Unfortunately, at least for a number of the people that have reported back to us, the products, written reports, usually disappear into files and filing cabinets never again to see the light of day (unless of course, something bad happens).

In the last five years, we have seen a growing number of professionals interested in using digital storytelling precisely as a way to make the product of the processes take on new meaning. Capturing one's professional process over the course of a year, as a classroom teacher, for example, with the idea of a multimedia project as the final assessment piece, provides a wide array of possibilities for the professional to explore. They can look at their relationship to the students through recording the students at work, their own awareness of developing new styles of teaching and testing new curriculum by documenting themselves as teachers, or they can find themes and issues around their personal life or the larger context of their school or district, that set the backdrop for a story.

With a grant from the Spencer Foundation, CDS worked with the National Writing Project (www.writingproject.org) to collaborate with a group of rural educators from around the U.S. in a project to encourage this kind of assessment, thought of as an extension of this particular group of educators' work as "teacher-researchers." The resulting stories have found their way into countless dialogues with other educators, as well has inspired numerous school districts to consider projects to capture the reflections of their classroom teachers.

With the story completed, in an environment of shared reflection, these artifacts can in turn inspire and lead to additional, and more in depth, reflections by their peers. The portfolio of the stories, (in our example for a school, or school district but it could be equally a large commercial organization), become a treasure trove of ethnographic detail. These multimedia stories can then provide an effective and entertaining way of presenting the arguments of administrators and managers about changes in organizational thinking.

Using digital storytelling in this way, particularly as these require the training of staff in new communication literacies at the moment, are not yet practical for a broad implementation, but as we said about the educational environment, you only need look a few years ahead with the next generation of professionals entering the market.

Job Preparation and Career Development

Our colleague Professor Glynda Hull, at UC Berkeley's School of Education, has done significant scholarship in the area of adult literacy in the job preparation and career development fields. She was also one of earliest converts to digital storytelling as a educational practice. As she explained to us, she could see the inherent value in multimedia tools for developing writing, but she also recognized the particular role that the personal digital stories could have in re-shaping identity.

In the work that she and her colleagues have helped to foster in the economically struggling communities of the East Bay, working with job training centers such as Urban Voice, there has been effort to examine how much the role of affirming one's life story through a digital story (in comparison to a written text) changes the attitude and success of the aspirant towards a new, perhaps more challenging career.

Our former Education Program Director, Caleb Paull, describes his findings and perspective on this particular issue in the interview in Chapter 12.

Team Building

During the height of the boom years of the late nineties, hardly a week went by without a national news story about how project management professionals were busy cooking up "experiences" for project teams to bond more closely. The examples included fire walking, rope courses, sports camps, extreme hiking, and skiing and rock climbing adventures, among many others.

Undoubtedly, people who are forced by circumstance to execute complex projects over intense periods will operate more effectively if they are initiated through an ego-stripping test of endurance and nerve. The physical test as a communal rite of passage is an ancient ritual.

But it would seem that the extremity of some of these experiences is perhaps a bit overstated for the relatively mundane application of the average professional project, no matter how stressful they become. They also seem much more suited to a traditional view of all-male cultures where physical prowess and leadership are considered interchangeable.

A number of our clients in both civic and commercial organizations have suggested that the strongest application of our work is in amplifying the process of the personal story exchange. While developing intimacies through personal stories is a common part of informal professional life, storytelling circles, and the more extreme production madness of a three-day digital storytelling workshop, gets to the heart of the matter much more directly.

Journalism

One of the surprising avenues for the exploration of digital storytelling in the last three years has been with journalists. It would seem that the journalistic profession is built on story. Ethical concerns in journalistic practice has tended to divorce personal emotional connection to story by the author. But for many of us, emotional content is at the heart of most effective journalism.

Our colleague Jane Stevens, a former New York Times and now independent science journalist, has developed her own approach and theories about new multimedia authorship for the journalist's profession. In this context she approached us to collaborate on a few workshops to train up some of her peers.

In our discussions with her, she suggested that the traditional divisions of labor between print, image and media journalists were dissolving in the context of multiple impacts of the dissolution of the journalist ethos as more and more news is developed as entertainment, the growth of online journalism and increased free agency among journalists, and the expectations of a much more complex relationship with audiences in the reporting of news because of interactive medias. She sees journalists as both multimedia storytellers, often with recognizable personal styles, and news facilitators, working with sources who will be developing their own outlets for stories to craft and execute those stories.

Digital storytelling is going to be a part of this process in some fashion.

Technology Training

Ironically, technology training, the most obvious application for the skill set we use, is perhaps the least interesting to us organizationally.

We realize that the digital divide exists along both socio-economic and cultural lines as well as age and gender. Getting access to the tool set is far from a closed issue, especially as the discussion expands globally north and south, and providing access is a critically important part of what our work should represent.

At the same time, we are not overly concerned about the ways innumerable communities that are seeking access will find their hands on the tools. As costs decrease, creative community solutions, such as community technology access centers in every school, church, neighborhood and collectives of homes, means the pooled resource can service a large number of people.

Digital storytelling is a great way to learn how to use a computer. We think that increasingly the approach of teaching office applications, games, and test taking programs as the first level of interface, will become more balanced as tools of web programming, photo manipulation, sound editing and video editing are seen as providing communication skills that work with, as well as above, the core writing, data management and manipulation.

We realize that we have not scratched the surface of the ways digital storytelling may become useful to various fields and endeavors, and we are always hearing about new contexts. In the fall of 2002, we launched the Digital Storytelling Association (www.dsaweb.org) to help connect practitioners of our practice together, and to hear more about their activities. We look forward to hearing your stories about applying digital storytelling in new contexts.

Interlude Four

Reasons to Believe

Why do some people endure great sacrifices? This is the story of my grandparents, Fernando and Emilia Sanchez.

When my grandfather arrived in Texas in 1944, he found himself, as many Mexican laborers did, Desenraizando la tierra. Clearing the Mesquite brush is perhaps one of the hardest jobs my grandfather ever did. My grandfather has spoken of the extreme heat that made his job nearly impossible.

Their workday that started at seven in the morning and ended at ten at night. His leather skin and his callous hands are evidence of the demanding nature of his work. His Patron, Rudolph Bell, was so impressed by Fernando's work that he asked Fernando to bring his family over from Mexico He promised them housing and work on his ranch.

The Sanchez family arrived in Ed Couch, Texas, in 1945.

However, things were not so easy. When the Sanchez family arrived, there was no housing ready for them. My grandmother speaks of how for several nights the family had to sleep on a flat-bed trailer. She speaks of how there was little defense against the cold mornings and the Sereno that would bring an unbearable chill to their bones.

My grandfather worked out in the fields for el Senor Bell seven days a week, from sunrise to sunset. My grandfather would even get his children to work in the fields to help finish the work faster.

For over 20 years, Mr. Bell compensated my grandfather with 25 dollars per week. My grandmother was paid two dollars per week for taking care of all the house chores and the cooking for the Bell family. The children were not paid for their services.

For over 20 years my grandparents saw their children grow up while they served el Senor Bell y su familia. My grandfather was completely devoted to his patron. After all, Mr. Bell had promised him 2 acres of his land, once he would have passed away.

When the Bell's 50th wedding anniversary occurred, my grandparents gathered as much money as they could and bought el Patron y la Mama the biggest floral wreath that was present at the Bell's 50th wedding anniversary celebration.

Rudolph Bell passed away in 1966. Shortly thereafter, the Sanchez family was ordered off their property by Mr. Bell's children. Fernando attempted to make his case that Mr. Bell had promised him 2 acres on his ranch. However, the remaining Bell family would not honor Mr. Bell's promise.

The Sanchez family once again had to start from scratch. Fortunately, Fernando had invested in some land in a quarter mile down the street. That's where they would settle down and start the rebuilding process, in the middle of a cotton field.

In 1975, Fernando retired after working another nine years for another Anglo farmer.

I've often wondered why Fernando and Emilia sacrificed so much of their lives by working out in the fields.

I think I now know why.

Muchas gracias por su gran sacrificio.

Su nieto, Ernesto Ayala

Sacrificios
—Ernesto Ayala

Although we have been at this work for 10 years, and traveled around the world teaching and sharing our methods, I have only had a couple of opportunities to return to my home State of Texas to teach our process.   In 2000, we received a significant grant from the W.K.K. Kellogg Foundation to assist with a program called Managing Information In Rural America. The program had the laudable goal of supporting grassroots community activists in designing and implementing technology-centered community development plans in a group of 24 pilot projects around the rural United States.

As luck would have it, one of the projects took us down to the Rio Grande Valley in far South Texas, to assist an organization called the Llano Grande Center. This organization, like many community groups, was primarily focused on the youth and education. They had tremendous programs in media, a radio station, youth advocacy, and college preparation. The college prep program was so successful that they were getting 20% of their seniors into out-of-state colleges including Ivy League and West Coast schools. Keeping in mind that the average family income was under $10,000/year and 80% of the parents did not have high school level educations, this was an extraordinary task.

In fact, at one point, there were so many Ed Couch students at the prestigious Brown University in Rhode Island, that they formed their own student group. More impressively, many of these students were coming back to teach and mentor their younger brothers, sisters, cousins and friends. One of these students was Ernesto Ayala, and as he shared the tale of his grandparent's life of labor and sacrifice, he captured a simple, but profound story.

Having grown up in Texas to parents who spent a large amount of time organizing Latino laborers into unions and working to defend and expand the civil rights of the disenfranchised throughout the South, I knew the Sanchez family story. And I knew the necessity of honoring their sacrifices and struggle for dignity.

In these stories, we look at our own life, our own values, and priorities. When we share them, we embrace history, even as we shape our shared future.

I can not imagine a more important role for our work.

11 Making Community

A Conversation with Thenmozhi Soundararajan

"Until lions have their own historians, tales of the hunt shall ever glorify the hunter."

—Ghanian Proverb

Culture is a Weapon/Strategies for Community Building

Thenmozhi Soundararajan is a filmmaker, singer, and grassroots media organizer. As a second generation Tamil Dalit/Untouchable woman, she strives to connect grassroots organizers in developing countries with media resources that can widen their base of resistance. From 1999-2001, she was the director and founder of the Center for Digital Storytelling's National Community Programs in which she developed the framework for community based digital storytelling. In that capacity she has worked with over 200 communities around the country developing new media practices for their work. Further, she is in residence at the MIT Center for Reflective Community Practice, writing about her experiences with community based digital storytelling. She is also a 2001-2002 Eureka foundation fellow. She has been featured by Utne Reader as one of the Top 30 Visionaries Under 30. Currently, she is co-founder and executive director of Third World Majority (TWM).

Joe Lambert: How did you become involved in digital storytelling?

Thenmozhi Soundararajan: I became involved with CDS in 1999 when I approached you and Nina after an open house about the possibility of being in residency at the Center or a possible internship. I was interested in addressing the ways to meld political film making, or facilitative film making, with an intentional organizing strategy. I did not have a fixed idea of what that would look like, it was a general value that I wanted to explore in the production process. I believed there was something urgent about this understanding and developing this practice in the new media realm was necessity not a choice.

One of great strengths of CDS is that you were very flexible in allowing the space for my experimentation to occur, and the openness for theory to develop from the field. As I became involved in touring and teaching workshops, we would go out, return, discuss, and reflect back on our experiences. This would allow us to become honest and accountable as a group and as a program about all of our methods.

The time that I was CDS' Community Programs Director was a critical time for me. Very few young people get the opportunity to be so quickly immersed in all the aspects of a given methodology, from the tutorials, to the story circle, to the production supervision.

JL: You approached that responsibility with a background in Third World filmmaking... What experience did you bring into the practice of digital storytelling from your academic work and your experience as a filmmaker?

© 1998 Thenmozhi Soundararajan.

TS: I have been involved as an artist and an organizer in an ongoing process of defining a theory for facilitative media that is informed by third cinema for over five years now. As a movement, Third World Cinema emphasizes using film and video as means of connecting other struggles for self-determination within the community. The idea is that film as a production entity is subject to the same values that are present and inherent in the movement in which you are participating. So where in mainstream media they operate with a hierarchy of director and crew operating separate from the community they are documenting, the popular Third World filmmaker would organize production based on non-hierarchal systems of accountability in collaboration with the community.

I also wanted to look at the notion of skills transfer in doing media and documentary work. If you look at the way anthropology or media ethnography works, you have a skilled professional from outside the community documenting the people's lives and stories. When production is complete, and the work is distributed, the audience may have a larger exposure to the issues within this community, but there is little or no transfer of capital or skills. Conceivably, the filmmaker is provided access to the financial support for future projects, greater access to markets, and awareness of opportunities. But the community, in the long run, does not receive these benefits. Even when some degree of training or skills transfer takes place, there is often little thought about how the work can be made sustainable.

And it would be harmful enough if this was how most disenfranchised communities experienced filmmaking, but in many of the places and with people with whom I work, there is a long history of trauma with the camera and in general with technology. So for my practice, and for the theory we are developing to inform this practice, we also need methods to create a safe space for members of the community to discuss these issues.

JL: When you say a long history of trauma, to what are you referring?

Whether it is the Internet or the camera, the computers and how we structure them, all of these technologies have particular legacies of colonialism, and military and police intervention. For example, the Internet, the original ARPA-net, was a direct result of a scientific and military collaboration to develop a communications system for times of military crisis in the 1970's. While part of this was related to Cold War concerns, it was also occurring in the backdrop of counter-intelligence and repression within many of the communities of color in the U.S. If you look at film and video, you just have to look at the role mainstream media plays in our communities. The images that are portrayed create negative stereotypes, but more insidiously, they promote passivity and powerlessness. In the longer historical sense, as the cultural critic Coco Fusco has commented, the camera was used for ethnography and anthropology as the first line of colonial engagement with Native populations. This trauma is remembered by people, even as it is re-inforced today by the fact that almost every part of our lives are now under surveillance with video cameras.

As a result it is a double-edged sword when you take on the use of media technologies in a grassroots context.

JL: Part of your awareness of these issues comes from your own political experience and your own cultural background and nationality. You have worked in the area of Dalit culture, the issues of Indian and South Asian culture, can you talk about how this affected your own work as a filmmaker and cultural activist?

TS: One of the reasons why I was so insistent about learning film and video technique is that many times people in different political contexts make media work the last priority. I am a second generation US citizen, from the Tamil Dalit people of India. We are at the very conservative counts at least 250 million people, almost as large as the population of the US. Yet very little is known about my culture and people, even in the context of South Asia. The reason why is that we exist as a community that has been oppressed for thousands of years. In India, you do not hear much about us because the media is controlled by the Brahmin press. Our voices and the media that has been distributed has come out through much hard won grassroots infiltrations.

For us to take our struggle to the next level we need to produce our own media, we need to be the ones that define what our own images are like, because all the throughout our history other people were defining who we were. We were given the name, Untouchables, by the Hindus, and given the name "Scheduled Castes" by the British. Who our Gods are, what our values are, and what defines *our* cultural heritage in their eyes has always been negative.

Much of our building a base of resistance included both the fight to reclaim our civil rights, like in the U.S. but also to reclaim our culture. This is why I am so drawn to that Malcolm X quote, "Culture is our ultimate weapon." Because once we take back our stories, cultures and values within our communities or nations, no matter what they do to you, they can't take back that essential sense of beauty that is you, and that is always your own. Fighting for your culture is fighting for your dignity. Perhaps more than ever in the current context of globalization and the globalization of culture based on the U.S. media's depiction of the world, we have to battle for cultural and political self-determination.

JL: Part of your perspectives grow from a perspective of a Third World youth, and the issues of young people vitalizing the current anti-globalization movement. Can you talk about your perspective as a youth activist?

TS: Young people have always been a part of movements. I want to resist the segmentation of a youth sector of the movement as being somehow exceptional. There is a perception, among funders for example, that youth deserve special support as long as they are youth. But as soon as they emerge as adults, the efforts to educate, expand their social consciousness, and connect them to their larger communities is somehow less important.

In the context of our media work, in the late nineties, we had the discussion of the "Digital Divide" in our schools and questions of access for youth to new technologies in our communities. It was approached that the computer was going to be a way of salvation, but without a thoughtful consideration of the ways that you integrate technology as part of the struggle to address the issues that are the bread-and-butter issues like welfare reform, rent control, police brutality etc., and what is the best way to build and support the cultures within the community. People were training community folks, especially in our schools and community technology environments, without an intentional curriculum and practice for how training should be adapted to a specific community practice. In effect there was a lot of damage done, and it put our youth and other members of our communities back into the abusive relationship to technology that mirrored the historical legacies of transgressions against these communities.

I feel like that is one of the areas that CDS Community Programs, and now in my work with Third World Majority, that our organizer fill a valuable space, of linking the values of the movement to the way you teach these technologies. That's why we choose the teachers that we do. That is why we show the stories that we show. We are very conscious about how we relate with each other, with ourselves, and with the technology.

One of the things that was really interesting was in the anti-globalization movement was the role of the independent media centers in providing alternative media coverage of the events of Seattle and beyond. We knew that we would not get that positive of mainstream coverage, so we said, "let's compile all the resources, all the knowledge and let's set up our own independent media networks." This model of movement-oriented, independent media networks has spread to over 20 countries around the world. Anytime there is a particular political flare up or crisis situation, within a couple of days there is an independent media center that brings journalists and provides equipment to cover the story. Their approach is to broadcast the voices of the people involved in those situations. I think that it has been very threatening to the mainstream media because many people are now going to these alternative news resources as their main source of unmediated news.

At the same time, the alternative media movement also has to address our own production standards, while our grassroots low-tech image was helpful in initially building trust with many communities, there is a larger struggle within the movement to incorporate high production values to help gain credibility with a broader audience. That is the next step of our work.

JL:. You talked about the values of community digital storytelling, can you talk what you think some of those values are?

Second part

TS: The main focus of our organizing strategy is how community folks can best learn the story and technical skills and make the program they create around their own needs self-sustainable. We have a facilitative training process, similar to the CDS structure, where there is a teacher and an assistant teacher, but we also make sure there is a community teacher that we are collaborating with, whose community wisdom is given equal weight to the "technical" knowledge of the other trainers present.

Another value we practice at TWM is teaching with curriculum that comes from the community we are working with. There are two parts to why we follow this concept. First, technology curriculum at schools and educational institutions has caused an incredible trauma within our communities because the textbooks, the software, and the hardware, are not built with the history and cultural context of our communities in mind. So when you are setting up a training environment, you have to be really deliberate about what images, sounds, and effects are presented, because people are already expecting to be shut down. So it is really important to have curriculum that comes from our communities' perspective—that speaks to our own ideas and the value systems that are embedded in the way we tell stories.

Secondly, stories are extremely different from community to community, from culture to culture, because they represent a collective wisdom drawn from implicit values not easily accessed at first glance. As we were talking about, some communities value non-resolution in story. In Western communities, everything is always about resolution. But in many non-western communities there is not the same insistence that the story have a definitive moral lesson or central insight. Accepting ambiguity is part of the wisdom of their culture. This sense of how stories are told is a vital connection to their entire approach to language and culture.

JL: Tell me about your new organization, Third World Majority?

TS: Third World Majority is a young women of color, political new media training center dedicated to global justice. As a collective our mission is to develop new media practices for radical social change that challenge the notion that a media organization cannot also do grassroots political organizing. Our programs explore the interrelated nature of politicized new media production that includes digital video, the web, graphic design, sound engineering, and animation. Through our efforts and collaborations with other organizations, we support organizing in real, representational, and virtual worlds

When we started TWM we had very few answers but lots of questions. Why do we feel uncomfortable around technology? Why is the culture of training and learning of technology so inaccessible? Why are all the techies we know white alpha-male assholes? Why are media labs, tech centers, and public access stations so often empty not used by communities of color, and why is the damn media democracy movement so white?

Clearly the first big step for our work was reframing a lot of approach to technology in the context of understanding its military and colonial legacy, but then we really needed to put our proactive vision out next. We recognized that first and foremost that since media spaces were places associated with past and current drama (including a host of service oriented techies who have only barely evolved from their well-meaning anthropological missionary counterparts from colonial times) that whatever we did in TWM meant that we could not build a physical lab for people to come in. Creating a technology space and then expecting that to become a "community center" is a ridiculous concept. There is nothing inherently built into a computer that engenders community building (in fact it is exactly the opposite). So with our first seed-grant we bought a seven-station portable G-4 laptop lab similar to the one I worked with at CDS. With the laptops, we could train in the spaces communities already felt at home, so we taught around the country in barns, churches, community centers, schools, and people's homes. With the technology portable and actually rather small, folks were able to focus on the Cultural products they were translating and reshaping in a digital medium rather than stress about the technology itself. It also prioritized for us the primacy of the community and the use of technology as tool and just a tool.

The other aspect of our teaching process was we needed to tackle was how to unpack the assumptions around the coded-boy's club nature around technology. As young women of color who had been early adapters of web and video technologies for the movements that we had been part of, we had all faced being shut out of labs, being condescended to by other techies, and learning the tools on curriculum that at best was not relevant or at worst was horribly offensive. We also realized that as working-class young women of color in a racist, sexist, classist society, our leadership and vision for our communities is always silenced (inside and outside of lab spaces).

So we began to rebuild the matriarchy literally. We prioritized the leadership of young women of color as our trainers and as our organizers, and tech support. When folks come to one of our trainings, one of the standard lines we hear is "Wow, I never have seen so many young women, let alone young women of color know what they are doing around so many computers!" "Yeah," I say, "and we even know how to program our own VCRs!" It's funny how so simple a shift of WHO is teaching is not a simple thing at all. Because, while it literally changes the face of who is training, the other thing that happens, is that I think relationships built within this context are also different. And while this is not to repeat stereotypes of gender binaries, but as an organization we are working towards modeling collective, intentional, nurturing models of leadership.

Finally, I think as young women, we assert and recognize the leadership women have had for a long time in our communities from mother to daughter, to nurture the passing on of our stories, culture, and traditions. This is an extremely important role young women continue to play, and we believe it is vital to recontextualize our work as not just technology trainings but spaces of our cultural resistance.

JL: Can you tell some stories about some of the contexts you have been doing your work?

TS: What comes to mind is the large project we just completed in conjunction with the Active Element Foundation, an organization that builds relationships between grassroots networks among youth organizers and artists, and hooks them up with funding sources and support. They approached us to assist them with organizing a major digital storytelling retreat with sixteen of their youth groups from around the country, as a state-of-the-movement gathering. The funding came at the last moment, and we had two weeks to find a place, locate the equipment, book the tickets, and organize the logistics for the event. But we did it and it was one of the most amazing experiences I have ever been a part of.

At this workshop, much of the politics were explicit and the focus on using the workshop for a reflection on the movement was a top priority. Many times when people come to a film and video workshop, or even in the short history of digital storytelling workshops, they think of it as a training opportunity. We said, yes, the training and skills transfer, and producing a finished story are important, but the collaboration and the story sharing was critical. We wanted to see the relationships build across movements, across issues, and between agencies, so we prioritized our time to insure that this could happen.

We used the workshop to provide a model for resistance culture in several ways. While we were teaching film and video, and showing great examples of digital stories, we also had people share chants, and songs from the different movements from around the country. People could then walk away knowing the issues of the struggles, but also know the values and the songs people sing to share and celebrate their resistance. We created a place where people wanted to share, stay up for late night cyphers (music/performance parties), in what was essentially, a week long cultural festival.

Then when we had the Saturday night public event, we had people go up and perform and do spoken word, introduce their pieces, and share songs. It was one of best weekends of my life, and several people came up and said that it had been one of their best weekends, because they had never had that space open for them, a space where hope was alive. We devalue the ways that culture creates political power. That is the biggest thing that we sometime forget, that culture is our hope, and if we lose that, we lose a lot of what is viable to shape the direction of our future.

JL: How were the teachers selected?

TS: We selected teachers that one, had organizing experience, that was the first priority. Secondarily, we had people with the digital storytelling technical skills. In most of our workshops, we are constantly developing the production skills in seasoned community organizers from our collaborating communities, so that those skills will remain in the community.

JL: What do you think is transformative for the participants in the digital story-telling process?

TS: So much of how we structure the workshop is influenced by popular education teaching methods. Popular education begins where people are, and in our workshops we begin with the wisdom people hold within themselves and in their stories. So for me the most transforming part of the workshop is always the story circle. The sacred and safe space offered within a story circle allows people to build empathy with the stories and each other, even when those issues are divisive and controversial.

Many times when you bring people from contrary positions in any other context around the world they are going to come out against each other from what they believe is their objective position on the issues. But within the story circle you reframe their relationship where they are both storyteller and listener. When you inscribe two people like that within the same narrative, that inscription builds bonds of solidarity, and builds relationships in ways that would not have happened before.

In the Active Element workshop we had youth from communities like the Bay Area, New York, Cincinnati, Selma, and Milwaukee. We also had folks from urban and rural contexts. There was this one particular moment, where one of the students, whose name was Life, was talking about the Cincinnati riots. He described the history of racism and segregation in Cincinnati, He said that when that stuff went off, and 16 people were killed, "you knew it was coming, knew it would happen, and it took us three minutes to take back a city, a city that had been taken away from us all the way along. And imagine," he said, "imagine if we were developed, imagine if we had each other's backs, if we were a movement, how little it would take to re-create the world in the way that we want." And people in the group said, "Yeah, imagine that, and imagine that, etc."

There were other youth from a group called Young Women United from Albuquerque that created this amazing piece about the violence that young women of color face in their homes, schools, and neighborhoods. The way they told the digital story was circular, and they all talked about what it was like to be young women of color facing the interlocking systems of oppression, but also how they resist together, their voices told in a round only doubled their story's power. And everyone was like, "damn, that's it." All the participants fed off the love and hope they gave each other.

There was this enormous release within the workshop because of the level of frustration that most of us feel in grappling with all the issues within our communities. The problems with the accountability of institutions in our community; the education system, the lack of economic sustainability, the criminal justice system gentrification, environmental justice... I mean the list goes on and on. At the same time, these young people are also involved in providing key leadership, connecting people, and mobilizing the resistance needed in their communities. So it was really powerful when the links were made in that story circle. And the links that were made from that excellent beginning were deepened throughout the rest of the workshop process.

If you are teaching the workshop with an intentionality around relationships and community building, you facilitate both for narrative and for relationships. It is a very subtle process in which that can happen.

JL: When you are doing a workshop, such as when we were working with one of the MIRA gatherings, there are subtleties that have to do with editorial decisions, leadership in collaborations, who remains voiceless in the collaboration, etc. Many times you can foresee the problems because you recognize the class, racial, or gender privileged attitudes of certain people in the collaborations, other times it is the subtleties of individual psychology.

Are these the subtleties you are addressing?

TS: These are all things that you would identify as a facilitator. Who is speaking in the room? Who is not speaking in the room? It also goes back further to the question of what license you are being given as a facilitator. If you have been asked to address issues of mediation and coalition building and you know there are difficult issues among the participants, one of the things I do, is show stories that would get to the issues even before the story circle. For example, if there are racial issues within a coalition, there are a set of stories that speak to different aspects of race relations from different contexts. So you set the stage for that process at the beginning when you are sharing and showing examples. So that by the mutual critiquing of the stories, it prepares people to address the issues in the story circle, and you can pull from references in the lecture.

Beyond facilitating to make sure that a discussion is not dominated by one particular view, the use of a team of facilitators also helps in that if the team has a unified approach, then you can decide who might be best to have specific discussions with a particular participant or group of participants.

JL: This means having the ability to customize the relationship with the participants with the strengths of each facilitator.

TS: Because of the "power" that people invest in teachers you have an ability to act as a neutral force to address contradictions or issues that may arise. For example, in the MIRA project in Taos, there was a woman who spoke of her frustration with the Anglo establishment. The story she told was quite eloquent but she kept putting her piece down. At the same time there was an Anglo in the group who was expressing to her that he felt her piece was negative. In this context, as the teacher, I could extend out an alliance between these two, by suggesting to the Anglo that while it is very hard to hear criticism, it is important and necessary to be open to understanding the impacts of privilege. I could then also tell the woman that it is never negative to speak the truth about your resistance. It is the recognition that only through listening and building alliances can the struggle move forward.

This sort of intervention can bring down the heat inside the room, but with an effective team of teachers, they can have additional conversations with people to go into greater depth around contentious issues raised in the story circle during the rest of the workshop.

To sustain this, you need to have consistent discussion between teachers to make sure you are aware of the group dynamic.

JL: You spoke before about the legacy of a colonial model in the way people relate to technology. Can you talk about how that manifests?

TS: To be totally honest, I think people lie. I think people lie to folks who bring technology into their community because they do not trust these people, and so they provide a surface of their perspective, but don't really get down to their real feelings and stories. That is why it is so important to have facilitators that they recognize as being from their community. As in, if you were working with Queer folks, having a Queer facilitator, or someone who is of a Native American background in the Native American context.

I think the other manifestation is about ownership. From the very beginning it should be clear what will happen with the stories and the images and material that are captured. Who will see the work and under what contexts? Because owning your wisdom and owning your images is something that was, and continues to be, taken away from many of these communities. So in a process like this, where you are trying to help people re-take control over the way their story is told as part of building their leadership, this needs to be explicit in the group discussions.

In the context of our program with Circle of Voices, a California Native digital storytelling project, we honored the sacred space of this gathering. What was discussed during the workshop was not to be discussed outside the workshop. Also, all of the material was removed from the machines, the participants had copies, but we did not keep secondary back-ups. Finally, the material gets to be defined and used by the communities first.

JL: Part of what I was asking is do you see an inherent issue about computing machines, and their design, and their relation to historical cultural attitudes and contradictions? In other words, is there an inherent contradiction between the general computing culture and doing empowerment and cultural work?

TS: I would break it down in a couple of ways. As I mentioned, there is the lack of trust within communities of people who have, in the last couple of decades, been offering computers in these various communities. In regards to the computers themselves, I think it is important to remember how toxic computer manufacturing is, and to keep in mind who builds these computers. Whether it is in the Third World or in the U.S, its is mainly women who are vulnerable to both the repressive labor practices and the unregulated toxic exposure they face in these high tech sweatshops. The computer designers, the computer engineers, who design these fancy machines, are not thinking much at all about the human cost of the manufacture. While computers are promoted as a green industry, they are in fact quite stained with blood.

I also think that the individualism of computer design is a reflection of the Western heritage. It is part of the legacy of consumerism where there is an expectation that people will use their technical devices in the privacy of their homes, alienating and separating people from each other. I think if you look at communities in the Global South where technology applications have been approached with a different perspective, the emphasis is on communal use, on ways that people share the resource and maximize the productivity for the community's benefit. Now in this culture the computer is built for a single user, but it would be so much nicer if you had ways that multiple users could design and integrate their work together in a relationship context.

This extends even to the color palettes and design motifs of the computer world. There is little sensitivity to different ways of seeing between cultures. Of course this is a reflection of who can currently afford the machines, but it also a particularly color- and culture-blind attitude that is particularly profound with the computer industry.

When you are teaching digital storytelling, you are quite aware that the software and hardware, are both built in a very real coded "boy" culture. And maybe more specifically, coded "boy loser" culture. So much about how learning is transferred isn't collaborative. It is about one-upmanship, about "oh, I have this, you don't, oh, let me show you this thing." It is very much about competition, and is antithetical to collaboration. This reflects a dominant culture male attitude, but it also reflects privilege: who has time or money to spend days keeping up with all of the cool new gadgets, latest websites, and hot software.

So now most people coming to any technical training, including the digital storytelling workshop, don't feel they can relate to this world, because the whole technology environment has designed to serve this narcissistic boy culture, who were in a position to be the early adapters and designers of this technology because of their privilege.

All of that said, the reason I am still doing the work relates to my attitude about literacy. In the short term, the way technology is set up is not particularly good for our people and communities. We are talking about maybe the legacy of this particular evolution in the culture of personal computing will be with us for the next fifty to sixty years. This makes it a critical time for us to advocate change in the very infrastructure of these technology systems within our communities and radicalize what it means for us to be global citizens. For us to become architects of the change in our understanding and use of technology, as opposed to compliant consumers, we need to be engaged as much as the dominant culture.

I think the community digital storytelling workshop is a really good introduction to this dialogue. It is a safe place where we can say, "ugh, we have to put up with this technology, it is necessary for us to engage, but we are engaged with an exit strategy in mind." If you fail to present this value system to people you are introducing to the computing world, then you are only perpetuating the attitude of inferiority and disengaged compliance toward adopting technology among oppressed communities. Which leads to the continuation of hostile mistrust, if not complete rejection, of those technologies. The same dynamics get played over and over again.

JL: Where do you think your work is going?

TS: I feel like story is at the core of all my work. It is what actually gets people beyond the technology, after the "ooo and ah" of the shiny expensive equipment, the thing that stays is the story. Story is the critical connection between personal subjective experience and larger political action, between individual and collective action. And for me I am still exploring how magical that discovery can be for individuals and their communities.

There is a way I want to see the movement grow where ultimately each community agency is its own hub of experience. They would use the stories not just for external communications and coalition building, but as a way that they maintain their history, their story, within the values and parameters that define who they are. They can use it to access past moments to inform current struggles.

For example, in the "Joe Gotta Go" campaign (The Selma, Alabama recent mayoral contest where a white mayor, who had served from the days of his opposition to civil rights in the 1960s, was defeated and replaced by their first African-American mayor), we did the piece, *Someone Died for Me.* It was an incredible externalization of how they do the work, why they do that work, at a critical moment in the campaign. They had been trying to get Joe Smitherman out of office for 37 years, and the struggle had truly come to a head in the summer of 2000. I had been assisting them with mainstream media work, trying to call attention to Selma through a series of op-ed pieces, press releases, and radio spots when the idea came of trying to do a digital story/music video based on an important song in Selma Civil Rights history that spoke of the tremendous sacrifices people had made to get the right to vote. They wanted to use this song to help people link the past struggle to that of the current voter fraud, and all the blocks the white establishment had put in front of the black community's disenfranchisement.

When we finally finished the digital story, we were in this big church, and the movie was going to be shown, and both the actor Sean Penn and the Black Panther activist Geronimo Pratt was there, and the biggest moment was not when the famous people spoke, but when the community saw those pictures. For people outside the South like myself, the pictures we used have an important historical interest, but for folks from Selma, the people in those pictures were their aunts, their uncles, their grandfathers, their grandmothers, friends, and other loved ones who had personally been willing to give their life to be free—and some did lose their lives. People were crying, people were moved, and I was truly humbled.

You cannot underestimate what we can do when we are fully connected to our culture and values. Three or four days later, because of their collective will and struggle, they won that campaign.

JL: That is a wonderful example. Whether or not the film becomes part of the legacy of Selma's struggle, or was just used for that particular moment, it is an incredible new gift to offer communities in these historical moments the tools to capture the emotions and perspectives of a struggle.

TS: It was incredibly important that it be seen, that it was three young woman of color who co-directed this piece, the other collaborators being another woman from Selma and a woman from Mali. It wasn't that the piece had been created by someone Sean Penn had brought from Hollywood, it was home-grown by people that generally would not have access, or be recognized for speaking up, let alone pick up a camera! I mean people still talk about it.

JL: Regarding the Internet, there is a protocol about honoring the sacredness of the story circle, that we have not found as easy way to publish or broadcast material that sustains those protocols. We do not have a mechanism via the Internet that invites people to be part of the experience, but can gauge the if a potential anonymous audience has developed the maturity or sensitivity that would allow them to understand the author's intent. An anonymous audience may not be able to contextualize the risks and vulnerability the authors of some of these pieces have taken. You have been approaching these issues, what are your thoughts?

TS: All of us have been struggling with what is the most effective way to distribute these pieces. Traditionally, when you created media, as independent media artists or as documentarians, your option for distribution was film festivals, public access TV, or targeted direct to video distribution to homes. Now we can also use the web and broadband connections to reach a larger but narrower audience. In most of these situations you cannot control the parameters of the audience and how the work is contextualized, which is important if the intention of the showing of the piece is to build community or encourage more stories.

JL: The problem for me is that broadcast, the notion of endless media that is pumped in and around our lives, is an inherently horrible cultural practice. While most media is filtered by our sense of interest and engagement, it is to one degree or another diminished by the noise of media ubiquity. We, as has been said, are a nation of neurotic channel surfers.

This creates an impossible system of valuation, because none of it feels relevant. We need circles of consideration, communities of context that provide stories, or suggest stories, that through their familiar relation to us, their knowledge of our life path and interest, can enlighten us. This is the idea of word of mouth, people say, "this story is relevant, you should see it," or put another way, "see it in this context, because I think it is relevant to you." I would much prefer seeing these stories travel by email, or locked behind a password and encryption, for which a community shares a key.

So part of our work is imagining beyond broadcast, and defining the terms of the ways that these authentic stories find their way to media environments. We are proud of our work with BBC-Wales because we think we have instilled a sense of seriousness, of caution, or sensitivity into the media professionals carrying out these community processes.

TS: I agree that we need these considerations. But what I would like to see is these dialogues not just be between entities of the Global North, or by experts coming from the North to "educate" the South, but to see exchanges promoted between representatives of one cultural practice in the South to another culture or community in the Global South. Can you imagine a training and discourse on digital storytelling between our friends in Mali and the Dalit community in India? The problem is funders do not see this as a necessity. It is very easy, relatively, to have someone from the First World to get funded to go south, have their transformative experience, and at the same time do a little to help the natives. It is almost impossible for experts in the South to get that same level of funding.

In terms of this work internationally, it is very important that the values and approaches of the teachers get examined, but also look at who is teaching, who is in the room. You have a few days to work with people, and people will definitely censor themselves based on the sense they are among people, that the leadership of the workshop would validate and defend their perspectives.

Going back to distribution, what we have been advocating for is looking at community based venues of distribution as a component of community building. We think community curation is the preferable option over external events, like film festivals. Partly because in the context of community curation the digital story can be produced with a whole series of other community cultural practices including, song, dance, spoken word, that sets the story in the larger framework.

We need to re-program our communities to connect with these community story venues, to make choices about whether to spend all their dollars on mainstream media or come see films about people they know, and through which they recognize their own story.

Because from the making, sharing, and screening of these pieces we are not just creating alternatives to the mainstream, we are creating our own lasting institutions, the beauty of which we discover story by story; community to community.

12 The Change Within

A Conversation with Caleb Paull

While in our daily lives we move between worlds in which our selves are different and even contradictory, in the authoring of self we make choices and negotiate between these selves that exist in different contexts and social worlds. From the reflective space of constructing story, in responding to and addressing the social worlds, roles, and codes of our lives, we can begin to form a sense of self-control, and a basis for self-direction.

Excerpt from *Self-Perceptions and Social Connections*
—*Caleb Paull, ©2002 All Rights Reserved.*

Dr. Caleb Paull, Ed.D, is a recent doctoral graduate of the University of California, Berkeley, School of Education. His dissertation, *Self-Perceptions and Social Connections: Empowerment through Digital Storytelling in Adult Education*, connected digital storytelling to discussion of educational philosophy, and the applications of the process in an educational setting. Caleb has been an educator for 10 years, having worked as a writing and composition teacher in his native New York City and in the Bay Area. From 1999-2001, he served as the Education Program Director of the Center for Digital Storytelling.

He currently lives in Chicago, Illinois where he works as a coordinator in Roosevelt University's Teacher Quality Enhancement Project.

Joe Lambert: How did you get involved in digital storytelling?

Caleb Paull: I became involved in digital storytelling through my graduate advisor at the School of Education in UC Berkeley, Glynda Hull. She had taken a workshop with other teachers in a writing program at Berkeley. And she had produced a piece about her childhood and her parents. In my visits with her every week, I would usually arrive and tell her I wanted to drop out of graduate school. On one of those visits she said to me, "Oh, I have to show you this thing that I made," and she tried to describe how she used photographs and she'd used music and made some kind of movie. I didn't really know what she was talking about. She put the videotape in the VCR and showed me her movie. I said, "Wow, that's amazing." I knew that was something I really want to do.

In high school, I ran a Public Access cable television show. I had a bit of experience in television and video at Brown University and after my work at Brown, but I had never worked with computer video editing. Video production had always been extremely difficult, and I relied on institutions that had huge expensive machines to do analog video editing. And Glynda said "Oh no, I did it all on the computer, in a few days." I thought if I could work that into my studies that it would be a reason to actually stay in graduate school.

As I recall I was taking a course at the time called Curriculum Studies and I thought this could be really interesting in terms of classroom uses and uses for teachers and their own professional development. So I decided to write a paper on the history of technology in classroom. What I found was that, historically, different technologies had been pushed into the classroom from above rather than in response to teachers' desires or needs. Consequently there was a history of resistance to technology by teachers, as technology often interfered with their classroom goals. The headaches of learning these new technologies and troubleshooting technical problems simple weren't worth it. Teachers for the most part have not felt comfortable with using technology themselves, which was reflected in how they imagined implementing it in their curriculum. At the end of the paper, I took a look at new directions in educational technology, directions that might be more meaningful and valuable in terms of teachers' and students' goals. I put digital storytelling out there as one of those directions.

About that time I called you and you offered me some material you had been writing, and by a happy coincidence the next semester, the Center for Digital Storytelling moved into the College of Education in Berkeley and offered its first course.

I've always wanted to be a screenwriter and a director and now I'm a teacher— let's see if I can meld them all together. So I took your class and the rest is history.

JL: Let's talk about your first experience doing a digital story-

CP: Actually, if I could do it over again I would do it differently. When I did my first digital story, I used a piece of writing that I had written as part of my work with the New York City Writing Project. It was a narrative poem that about my experiences with my father's poker games when I was a child.

I don't remember if I felt very stuck with writing at the time, or perhaps I was so locked in to the type of writing that I was doing for graduate school that I was hard for me to create an original piece for the digital storytelling class. But this older piece worked, and I really wanted to use it to experiment visually with the writing. Particularly, when I think of my relationship with my father, it has always been based on enjoying films together.

JL: You have been interested in the writing process as a means at exploring identity for quite some time. Can you speak about how this background shaped your interest in digital storytelling?

CP: I'd been teaching writing, and writing myself, and saw writing as a way of reconstructing experience, and making sense and meaning out of one's life. But when the writing entered the realm of digital multimedia, I saw a number of new possibilities.

For example, on the story about my dad, when I wrote the piece, I was not thinking about our shared interest in film. The story was a nostalgic look back at childhood and the importance of being part of this community of men. When I was faced with "how do I represent this visually?" I started to have new insights about other connections between me and my father. To represent poker visually, I brainstormed the idea of a number of films that have scenes of men smoking, of trails of smoke floating in the air. I realized that's an additional level of meaning. Drawing on these movie clips, it could speak to my father as the audience, beyond the original text, communicating this shared bond around movies.

I remember these particular scenes that we saw together when I was a child. So it was also a recollection of our shared relationship. So beyond my original attempt to just reflect on my impressions on my father's male community, the digital story came to inform the way that I construct the basis of my relationship with my dad.

JL: Digital storytelling is about individual insight, but it is also meant to be an effective group process. What did you see in this first experience regarding the effect on the larger classroom?

CP: I was excited by the whole process. There was an unbelievable excitement about this approach, particularly within the context of school and graduate school. People were coming and going in the lab, working hard on their projects. They would share what they were doing, and I would show them pieces of my work. And we give each other super-positive feedback, and it was genuine.

I've been in classes where the norm is saying something positive, just before you tear them apart. But in the digital storytelling class, we were all trying to tell stories that were important to us, and we all faced the challenge of working creatively with unfamiliar tools. So there was a lot of leaning on one another, and mutual support.

Also I was older than many of the other students, and at a different point in thinking about my own identity. I saw undergraduates approaching telling their digital story in a somewhat defensive way. It was as if they were saying, "okay I really don't want this to be that much about me, I'm not that comfortable with me, so I'm going to make it humorous or offensive or shocking."

Having that time in the class together and seeing where different people were willing to go, what they were willing to share, the strides that they took from the beginning to the end, was very revealing. Whether the final story was a deeply personal story or not, I still came to know them better. We could listen more honestly to whatever story that was being shared.

JL: So as luck would have it, we were able to hire you and put you on the road with our training approach. Can you talk as an educator about the way you viewed the methods of our workshop practice?

CP: To be perfectly honest, it's a little bit hard to take myself back to before this massive amount of work I recently completed about digital storytelling, so let me speak about how I look at it now.

JL: Yes, your dissertation has run over your brain.

CP: The environment that I first experienced digital storytelling was a semester long process. This is completely different than the CDS three-day workshop. At first, when I began to participate in the local workshops, both as someone creating a story, and someone assisting people, I thought "this is great;" three days, it's intense, it brought me back to teenage longings for these intense moments with people where people get to know each other. "Let me open myself up to you, you open yourself up to me, it'll be great."

And the three-day workshop is great. People have no choice but to get to know each other, and trust each other, and to take chances. The immersion allows the participants to go much deeper into the process than if it were a classroom that met two hours, once a week. You experience levels of exhaustion and epiphany that I think you might not otherwise attain.

At the same time, what came to be very frustrating was that it was such a short space of time, then it was over. The longer that I assisted in these workshops, and started leading them, the more I felt that there was such a powerful base that was built and then it was being left behind. In some cases, some of the people would take their experience to another level, and do something with it. This was true when they would have sufficient support where to help them to continue.

But in a many cases this amazing experience happened, and a skill set was built, there was a big wonderful celebration. Then it's over, and the participants go back to work on Monday.

That was very frustrating to me as a teacher, as an educator, and I imagine, in many ways, it was very frustrating to many of the participants as well.

I would imagine a year after one of the workshops, many people feel like it is really cool that I have this CD or movie, I can always show it to people, and be proud of that and say "I did this, this was great." But I don't feel that they could have fully explored how the whole process could have informed their personal or professional lives beyond the workshop.

JL: I agree with you. But the irony is that we have found that in principally servicing professionals, three days is an extraordinary luxury. To leave your job, and immerse yourself in a focused creative process, even if it directly relates to training and professional development, happens once a year, once in five years, for most professionals. We would like to imagine reflection is built into professional practice, but in difficult economic times, we do not think we can easily expand this program to more days. As for follow-up, and seeking ways to integrate these practices into the day-to-day work of professionals and enthusiasts alike, this is where we see the need for much more curriculum development.

In working with classroom teachers, with educators, what are some of the applications you can imagine for this process?

CP: As a starting point, I think there are a number of considerations in implementing digital storytelling in an educational context.

First, teachers are tired. Teaching is a tiring profession. It is very emotional. Teachers are also tired of technology, as I said. Technology has been pushed into the schools from above for years upon years. And rarely with any thought about as to how it would really integrate into actual classroom practice, or what teachers actually wanted to do, or about how it impacts the relationships within a classroom that are so important.

My experience with teachers coming into digital storytelling is that they assume it is yet another technology program they are being sold, and they have a healthy skepticism about it.

But the teachers I have worked with, they're very good at telling their stories. Very rarely do people ask for their stories, and so just the act of asking is very powerful. So when you start with a story circle, or sharing initial writing samples from exercises, and demonstrate what you are really interested in is their story, not selling them a new toolbox, they take interest.

And just the act of sharing those stories is the single most important part of a professional development experience, because it's creating community and a reflection on practice.

In making digital stories, teachers are given a new way to be creative. Creative artistic expression, particularly in the context of work, is not very encouraged. It is fun. It's not just "I gotta write an article for this journal about being an English teacher, teaching reading to third graders." It's what interests me, what excites me, and how I can bring it in the context of the classroom.

I can speak for myself, and I think for many teachers, that one thing that makes teaching such a wonderful profession is the vitality of the classroom. It's the voices of the classroom, it's the images of the classroom, (and) it's the energy of the classroom. In normal processes of talking about that classroom, researching that classroom, and sharing the story of that classroom with other teachers, you're usually relying on words to communicate what is really a daily multimedia experience.

To be able to take the actual artifacts of the classroom, to show that story, to be able to take the student's voices, the student's work and frame it all by what it all means to them; this is whole other order of magnitude of understanding about the classroom experience.

I don't think the process of classroom inquiry, of the role it can play in our schools, has been fully explored. Teacher ethnography is about collecting the pieces, collecting the artifacts, having some question in mind, and based on the question gathering all these things, but not being sure what story they're going to hold. In the gathering of these things, the question gets reshaped and the story begins to form, and in the telling of the story new insights are discovered about the classroom and eventually avenues for new stories open up.

And that's what I've seen happen with the teachers I've worked with, where they're both re-energized about their teaching, because they're taking themselves back into the classroom, and they're expressing it in this way that they've never been able to. They too begin to discover ways in which they can make meaning out of these classroom experiences that they might not have thought of before.

But they also discovered that they can produce something that brings a whole new audience into the discussion about what's important about teaching, and what's important about their classrooms, and what's acceptable to parents, and other teachers, and to the students in the classes.

JL: Story is a much more effective repository of data than many research methodologies that use data points as metrics. But how can we expand the use of story as a research and assessment tool for educators?

CP: I am exploring digital storytelling as an action research tool, an iterative tool where the points of reflection develop a professional portfolio. The idea is to return to your earlier story, again and again, in each iteration, and have that shape the research questions and artifact collection over many semesters or years. I think that it can be very powerful. It hasn't been done.

When teachers do this work and have a way of coming together around it, it goes beyond just individual reflection on one's own practice, it develops a community of reflective professionals. It should be part of what teacher's are doing anyway.

JL: Talk about your application of digital storytelling in adult education.

CP: My background is in adult education. I've always worked with populations and individuals who enter the classroom timidly and not feeling that they have a lot to contribute. So much of my experience of digital storytelling was people's sense of excitement and discovery about the stories that they could tell and how they could tell them.

I've done work with remedial writing and so the struggle was that students would enter these classes being told that they were not good writers, and writing is not fun for them. They don't feel comfortable taking chances and exploring their own voice. The process of digital storytelling broadens the definition of writing. With multimedia authoring, the student does not feel they are creating something out of nothing. At anytime you can't think of a word, you can look for a picture, and maybe that picture will spark a word or sentence or a paragraph. When you've exhausted your images, you listen to music and it offers other possibilities.

That's a big part of what interested me in the first place, let the students who don't feel that there are opportunities to tell their stories, and even when I try to give them opportunities to tell their stories it's a struggle, let's give them all the tools and permission possible.

One my favorite experience in working with CDS was my role in the Institute for the Future workshop collaborating on a story with three students from a, as they put it, "messed up" high school in East Oakland. Here were three students who felt they weren't receiving any kind of education in school, who were in the midst of a larger group of kids at the workshop who had been given tremendous validation for their writing in their schools. These three felt "we can't write like them" and therefore didn't write anything at all for the first week. Because of this fear of and struggle with writing, they seemed to believe that they didn't have important stories to tell.

To be able to sit down with them and say you do have a story to tell, tell it! And to have them speak and be able to record it and have their editing process be "let's listen back to our voices and choose the pieces that seem most important." Well that is what you do in writing, but it's suddenly there is a new option. They would say "Hey, can we use movies that we really like?' I would respond, "yes you can." Then they go, "Oh cool, there's this movie with this great scene." As it turns out that scene really represents a lot of what they're telling in the story.

All those avenues for expression were have validated my interest in digital storytelling. In addition, adults coming back into education are often seeking new definitions and new identity and seeking concrete changes. They're choosing to come to school for some sort of transformation. To have them go through this process where they can use all these tools to explore why they are here and what is important in their lives and tell that to themselves and others is really important and empowering.

JL: What are some of the other revelations that have occurred to you in your research and practice?

CP: In doing media work with students, I expected the process would engender self-empowerment. That had been my own experience and I would have been surprised if the students came out the process without it. What surprised me more was the sense of audience.

Our experience is that a movie is public. Our students had a sense of the public nature of the piece as they were creating it. They were thinking about how the piece could help or influence other people in the community. One person telling a story about immigration to the U.S., and the transition to life in this country, led to them thinking about how such a story could be a great help to others going through similar processes. I wasn't giving them that as a direction in their writing and producing the digital story, they were not instructed that the story had to serve a larger public purpose. I'd never seen that happen with writing. Unless I specifically made that part of assignment in writing, students would assume the discourse was private, or with me as the teacher, or at most with the classroom.

But with digital storytelling, the public role of their writing became part of the process—to have a social consciousness of their work. It brings a community together. Their sense of empowerment was not only having taken control of their own experience but it let them feel that they could face anything and that they were better writers.

In addition, creating a digital story takes people into an intense writing revision process. A much more careful critical reflection is required with the introduction of images and music, will these words fit these pictures, have I written too much, can the picture express something more effectively than my prose, or does my writing need to tell out what is missing from the image. And of course, the visual editing process is also filled with revision, trial and error, and discovery. A student looking for a picture can search through 300 pictures before they find the right one and they know it when they find it. And that's a powerful process of revision, of editing, of trying to get it just right.

I have barely begun to explore how to teach more traditional writing through the creation of digital stories as opposed to create digital stories out of writing. For example pivotal moments, detailed writing, how to bring the reader into the moment—it has a powerful potential.

13 When Silence Speaks

A Conversation with Amy Hill

Amy Hill is a video maker, public health consultant, and organizer with ten years of experience working in community and health settings to end violence and abuse. In collaboration with the newly formed Third World Majority, she has been coordinating Silence Speaks: Digital Storytelling for Healing, Resistance, and Violence Prevention, which provides violence survivors, witnesses, and prevention advocates with the opportunity to create short digital videos about their experiences.

Joe Lambert: How did you get involved in digital storytelling?

Amy Hill: I came to this work at a point of frustration with the limitations in the approaches to media education that I saw in the domestic violence prevention field. Most of this media work was formed around didactic classroom presentations and curriculums that did not speak to the actual experiences of the victims. When I found about digital storytelling, I thought that it would be an effective way to develop and incorporate visual media into community education and public awareness campaigns related to violence against women.

As I understood the arts therapy potential of digital storytelling, which was over my first several experiences in making digital stories, I came to see that digital storytelling could provide a transformative experience for victims of domestic violence.

JL: When did you first make a digital story?

AH: My first experience was with the Digital Clubhouse Network, which I found through the research and consulting I was doing for domestic violence agencies to identify interesting uses of technology for capacity building. They still under-utilize technology and computers in general, so I was looking for an interesting way to engage them that wasn't as dry as introducing them to basic software applications. So I stumbled upon the DCN on the web, and spoke with them, and they put me in (a) workshop that was specifically for non-profits agencies.

The DCN methodology is a bit different from CDS. They had the participants teamed up with a young person that handled the production work on the computer. The participant wrote the script, brought the pictures, and provided direction for the edit of the movie.

What I took away from the Clubhouse experience was two key things. One is that in telling my own story about my own experience with violence I realized that we needed to have workshops dealing with those specific issues. My comfort level was not very high in dealing with the subject matter in the context of a larger, more generally focussed environment. The second point was realizing the importance of directly empowering the participants in the use of the technology—to have them produce the pieces. My understanding of the strength of this approach came as I began working more with CDS.

JL: In your own experience, why do you think digital storytelling is useful as a reflective practice?

AH: There are a couple of things. From the perspective of working in the field of violence against women there is a fair amount of media that is presented in the guise of health education, and prevention, that end up as these canned, unrealistic scenarios. Most people in the field do not find that helpful. In having gone through the process myself, and having told my own story, and having coordinated a series of workshops with survivors and witnesses and people that do this work, there is a level of authenticity that comes through in the digital stories. It has a way of connecting other people. The digital story presents what a person that has been affected by violence has experienced in a way that the more dramatized, and canned approach does not.

Because I work with a number of domestic violence agencies, we end up working with staff members. In these agencies we have a great deal of discussion about how you draw the line between working directly with survivors and working with staff in setting up the workshops. What I have found is that the line is actually gray and blurry because a number of people that work in the field actually have some direct experience with violence in their own lives. Because staff members in these agencies understand there is such a great need for their services, they work a million hours for little money, we found is that across the field they don't have much time to reflect back on how their own experience affects the works that they do. Nor do they have time to step back and look at their experience in a way that provides for their own cathartic transformation.

In working with people at different agencies it has been enormously powerful for them. It has been an amazing team building experience. And where we have brought together representatives from numerous agencies it has also been an effective cross-agency support building process. People have told stories across a broad spectrum of issues related to violence; from human rights work in Colombia, to a young man works at Men Overcoming Violence who told a story about his own involvement in gangs, and how that informs his work as a youth guidance counselor. This spectrum of story allows people to make connections regarding the way different forms of violence are related.

JL: What do you see is unique to your approach to digital storytelling? As you moved toward a therapeutic practice, what sort of ethical and political questions did you have to address?

AH: Fortunately we have done enough workshops to have a body of work to begin to assess these issues in a way that I believe can make this process sustainable. As for the therapeutic benefit, the best way to express this is through an example from what someone said after participating in one of the workshops. A participant said that the workshop experience allowed him for the first time to have complete control over the telling of a story that related to a situation over which he had no control. So it was a way of reclaiming your own experience that allows you autonomy and agency in how you portray it back to the rest of world. That is a general feeling about the process and how it can be intensely cathartic.

People who participate in these workshops generally self-select. In other words, the workshop attracts people that have already gone through therapy and done some work with their issues and so this process takes them to a different level. It is one thing to sit with a therapist or in a group therapy session and just talk about their experience, but it is something all together different to put words to the experience, create a visual treatment of it, and incorporates music, and all the multimedia elements. It gives a person multiple levels of meaning to work with and describe the experience.

JL: What about the participant's sense of social agency, do you think this shapes their sense of contributing to the struggle against violence?

AH: Yes, most people experience a radical change in the idea of what they are going to do with their story project, from when they first hear about the project, to when they arrive and are oriented for the workshop, and again it changes as they move toward producing their piece. As teachers, we make sure that their decision about how to use the piece is always completely up to the participant in terms of what context that they want to show it in.

As a testament to their commitment of it having an impact on the world, we have found that most people are quite comfortable with us using the pieces on the website, or compilation tapes, or different community settings, conferences, film festivals. People have even said that they would be quite comfortable to be part of a community screening as a fundraiser, etc. They see it as a way to showcase their work and to stimulate more community dialogue about the issues.

I can say that whenever I have presented the work, or from the Silence Speaks website, the response has been hugely supportive from the constellation of professionals dealing with violence.

JL: Even in our public workshops, people are willing to take risks with emotional material, and ordinarily they are prepared for the emotional impact of this work, but sometime they are not. How do you address people's potential for going into crisis as part of the workshop experience?

AH: This is an important part of our learning from our work in the last two years. In addition to self-selection of participants, we make sure they understand that the workshop is not appropriate for someone currently in crisis or coming out of crisis situation. We make that clear in our materials and what we say to would-be participants or agencies representing participants. In addition we have worked with social worker with a history of working with groups to develop a self-assessment question for potential participants to think through whether they feel prepared to participate.

The questions include: Have you told the story before? What was your experience when you told the story? What kind of support do they think they might need in the context of the workshop or beyond? Asking people how they are going to feel in sharing their story in the context of the workshop or beyond. We also ask about their background with computers, so we can assess this?

While we indicate that none of us are licensed therapists, we have a great deal of grassroots experience in the field, for example, I am certified as a rape crisis counselor, we want them to assist us in this assessment.

We did a collaboration with a program of San Francisco's Women Against Rape which has a writing program called Fearless Words, which works with survivors of sexual assault. For that program, one of the facilitators for the writing component was a social worker that had experience in working with groups and she was part of our project. She could be tapped to provide support if anyone needed, and there was another representative of SF Women Against Rape that played that role as well.

In terms of curriculum adjustments, the biggest difference is that for the three-day workshop, we spend twice as much time on the story circle. We need discuss more and process more, so we reduce the lecture and tutorial sections.

With workshops with women, or specifically women of color, we make sure the instructors are all women or women of color. This creates a safe space for people to participate and open up around issues.

JL: Do you have an intuitive assessment of how your experience in working in these therapeutic contexts might be relevant to other areas of the health professions?

AH: We feel that our work in digital storytelling links directly to the traditions of narrative therapy and art therapy, about which there is substantial research of its positive effects on recovery. Narrative therapy has addressed both the general power of re-writing the life story you carry with you, as well as the specific impact that the writing process has in reflection and feedback in a therapeutic environment. Art therapy addresses creative expression in general.

JL: I had the experience early in our digital storytelling process of working with an incest survivor that was particularly poignant to me. I realized that for a survivor, going through the family album was a painful journey into a territory of denial that was represented in the snapshots of happy family gatherings. In the specific piece, there was a photo of a parent, the father in this case, who was the abuser, and the image captured in the body language of the child, and even the expression on her face, a sense of separation and distance. In working on her edit, the survivor was able to deconstruct that image, to call attention to details, and take control of the meaning of the image in a new way. And as she talked about her experience in the film, her voice added another layer of depth and complexity. It was enormously powerful.

AH: There is a wonderful book, *Home Movies and other Necessary Fictions*, by Michelle Citron, a feminist filmmaker and theorist at the University of Chicago. She made a film in which she took home movies from her family and re-explores power dynamics in her family. It was her way of taking ownership in a production sense that had situated her as a child on the other side of the camera. So she twists this around and takes on the role, in this case, of her father, who was the one with the camera.

While she was a professional and had training to do this, digital storytelling is allowing anyone to use similar tools to explore a very similar process, to re-examine, and reclaim and explore the aspects of their experience. In that sense, I think this is really groundbreaking.

There is also a way in which some of the modes of art therapy and narrative therapy can also be inappropriately clinical, and not very accessible in a community context. This can turn off many young people, and particularly women of color. As such, there is a little hesitancy on our part to align too closely with the therapeutic arena because we see what we are doing as more grassroots, and culturally relevant.

JL: In that sense it relates more to the notions of co-counseling and peer counseling movement that have tried to position themselves not as opposition to the professional medical priesthood, but as effective alternative for a large number of people.

Are there other adaptations in your practice?

AH: In terms of comparing experiences, there are two key things in the past year. One, in the project with Women Against Rape, we met as a group for two hours for eight weeks prior to the three-day workshop. This allowed for the time in space to get to know each other and bond as a group, as well as develop scripts. I also did the storyboarding session in advance. We also had an art night where people did artwork, that people either did or did not use in their final pieces.

Then everyone came into the workshop with a developed idea of their script as well as fairly developed sense of the storyboard.

So what that showed me was that the three-day crash course by itself is not particularly appropriate for survivors. There is enough anxiety about the technology component alone, that it became much more gratifying to me, as well as the participants, to rationalize the larger commitment of time and resources. The stories also were more thoughtfully developed and almost everyone succeeded in completing a story. So I think this preparatory process is a more ethical approach for working with the issues that these survivors are facing. I am now integrating this idea, of a four to eight week preparatory process into the proposals I am submitting.

The limitation is that this works for a local practice, but not one in which we are trying to work with people in communities outside the Bay Area. We cannot imagine being away for these extended period, and it means we would have to trust our collaborators in another area to facilitate this whole portion of the experience.

The other learning experience we had was teaching a workshop with an organization in Arizona called Tuba City for Family Harmony with Navajo and Hopi Women. On the other end of the spectrum in terms of preparation, we were working with women who really could not come for three days, with issues of jobs, childcare and transportation. So we re-thought the workshop, and fortunately we had a small number of participants, we were able to work one-on-one as couselors to develop stories. They recorded their script, and did the edit, but we assisted with production, such as the Photoshop process.

The Tuba City workshop also addressed other issues of our process because it seemed more complicated to look at the issues of domestic violence with people from communities that are carrying such a profound historical grief around genocide.

And finally, one participant also had a low level of English language literacy. While she was able to develop a story, it was difficult for her in reading and recording the story. So that suggests more ethical considerations about how we would work in environments with adults who have limited literacy since so much of the work is formed around writing.

JL: There are a number of ethical considerations when you are working in resource-poor environments, and I think we have to be quite thoughtful about how the collaborators and the digital storytelling teachers communicate with participants about expectations, follow-up and the use of the stories. It is not a small irony to bring 21st century tools into environments that have 19th century infrastructures.

AH: Toward the future, we want to find a way to use the work in a broader context of community organizing, and to develop more consistent follow-up with the agencies we have worked with so we can figure out how to use the work on an ongoing basis.

Part of this is driven by the current media environment that continues to be filled with gratuitous images of women in positions of victimization and being terrorized. Not only that, but the approach of the so-called "women's" television that ends up portraying women as constantly being victims of stalking or domestic violence in this weird and creepy way. We feel compelled to put out a different version, people's real experiences, and create media that is driven by women and women of color that are so often under-represented or mis-represented in mainstream media.

So being able to provide the transformative personal experience and provide access to tools in a way that simply would not work in other media access centers. This is what is powerful. The stories that have been created simply would not have been shared in a general digital video class.

JL: In thinking about this discussion for the book, it seemed that the lessons of this work would be relevant to discussions about doing work in the context of disability, life threatening disease, hospice care, etc. What are your thoughts on how this relates?

AH: Silence Speaks frames its work about the issues of violence and abuse, but people have responded to this in a number of ways. I think it is inappropriate to provide a stipulation to people that you must tell a story that is about an overt form of violence. As such people have told stories from a number of angles that are more generally about healing. One woman made a piece that was tribute to her brother-in-law who died of AIDS. People have done stories about pregnancy and motherhood, sexuality and body image, which has a clear relationship to a history of violence and abuse and yet they are expressing this whole other constellation of issues.

Going back to the original impulse of this work, it is also about a strong belief in the power of art in the process of social change. When I go back and look at what inspired me, and motivated me to take action and get involved, it has usually been art. A key part of our work is creating beauty out of situations that are not at all beautiful. In that way in touching people at a core emotional level that will lead them to think in a new way and perhaps get involved and take action.

JL: Some place there is a core theory in this work, related to the larger cultural democracy and arts and social change movements, in which there is an understanding that when people experience trauma, violence, oppression, that part of the process is a de-signification of their lives. The loss of power in being brutalized reflects itself in people feeling invisible. There is a feeling that there is no "sign" of their existence, which others in their families, their communities, their social world, need to heed. Cultural work is about re-signifying people, giving them tools to declare the value of their existence.

For better or worse, in our culture, there is a hierarchy of signifying presentation. At the top of that hierarchy is the screen; television and film. What I have seen is the actual lifting of spirit that occurs as people see their images, hear their voices, and connect their story to the medium of film. It is a particular dynamic or power, that I don't believe is achieved in dance, music, theater, writing or visual arts presentations. It is perhaps regrettable that these historic forms have been diminished in their significance as communications media in our culture. But, as my friend Guillermo Gomez Peña has jokingly suggested, the new existential question is "TV or Not TV."

There have always been people that recognized this, filmmakers and video artists, who have gone up the training and technical ladder, and found the large financial resources to express themselves in this media, but the idea that filmmaking can be a general literacy, available to the mass of people, which is possible with the advent of this toolset, is profoundly different.

AH: Which is why a lot of filmmakers don't really know what to make of this work, and in my experience, are threatened by it, because it really breaks down the distinction between the people who are the creative professionals and the rest of us.

JL: Again we are talking about a relationship between the lay practitioner and a priesthood? The priesthood is very aware that its power is predicated on the obfuscation of the knowledge that they have. And obviously, we do not think this knowledge is mystical.

AH: Popular education practice is relevant here. In developing their own story and listening to others, people can make the links between their own struggle and the larger social struggle. Individual stories add up to the larger story. By starting with your own story and analyzing your own problems, a larger social consciousness is possible.

JL: But in doing digital storytelling we are saddled with the inelegant, feature ridden, toolset that is regrettably laden with the dominant cultural male attitude of the more toys, the more bells and whistles, the more value is invested in the tool.

AH: Which is why this work is so important with women and women of color because clearly a technophobia exists because of the perception that this is a male domain, and the fact that technology has been used against us in the past.

JL: Final thoughts?

AH: I feel that the work we are doing in helping to provide a transformative experience for survivors of violence links us to one end of the spectrum of the movements for social change. Being victimized by violence is a human rights violation. Allowing survivors to speak and have their stories heard heals all of us. And as we are healed, we can perhaps heal the world from its own cycles of violence.

14 Emotional Branding

A Conversation with Dana Atchley
© Joe Lambert/Dana Atchley

As discussed in the first chapter, Dana Atchley's work, *Next Exit* is one of the critical wellsprings of the digital storytelling movement. For a the decade of the 1990's, he toured and worked tirelessly to bring people together under this banner. In 1998, I was able to have a conversation with Dana about his work, and some of his experience in working with companies.

His work in the corporate sector was quite broad. As a presenter, he was a key-note presentation at dozens of corporate functions and trade shows. Along with a number of collaborators, in 1997-98, he designed the Digital Storytelling Theater for the World of Coca-Cola, Las Vegas. He worked on corporate presentations with Douglas Ivester, the CEO of Coca-Cola®, and Bill Dauphinais, a vice president at PricewaterhouseCoopers. His other clients included Hallmark Cards, EDS, AT Kearney, The Institute for the Future, Apple Computer, NCR, Adobe Systems, Grocery Manufacturers of America, J. Walter Thompson, Pinnacle Systems, Intel, and Silicon Graphics.

Dana Atchley passed away in December of 2000. The work of Dana Atchley Productions has continued with his wife, Denise Atchley, as director.

Next Exit

Joe Lambert: How are we differentiating the concept of digital storytelling from the more general idea of multimedia?

Dana Atchley: By putting the word storytelling in there, you shape the brand.

Storytelling is the key ingredient. We are telling stories.

Stories mean many things to different people. You and I have been talking about the anecdotal nature of conversation, the use of stories in informal presentations. Conversational storytelling is the kind of storytelling most of us are comfortable with and understand.

When we refer to digital, we are talking about a utility … a tool. We have been given a new set of tools to create and share our stories. The tools are extremely diverse; there are the software, the hardware used, and the actual publishing and dissemination media.

JL: Do you think we are also talking about integrity? I believe we use digital storytelling in the same way the film community uses independent film. Independent has come to mean more than "outside of the studio system." It is work in which the director's or screenwriter's narrative voice is sustained. Similarly, in a culture where digital becomes synonymous with special effects and the generic narratives of games, we use storytelling to ground the use of digital tools in the search for meaning.

DA: I wouldn't try to over-define digital storytelling because it can be inclusive of many different kinds of work. I think you and I are most compelled by work that shares honesty and integrity, and has an emotional basis for its message.

JL: *Next Exit* is an inspiration for many people. What makes *Next Exit* effective?

DA: First of all, it is honest and emotionally resonant. Secondly, *Next Exit* has a pool of 60 stories from which I can draw. Each story stands on its own, but they also interconnect and combine in numerous ways.

Next Exit is set in an engaging framework. I think people love seeing the campfire. It suggests the shared participation of all the observers. Every storyteller should start with something like that, something that establishes your relationship to the audience in an evocative way.

JL: In storytelling, as distinct from theater or public speaking, the storyteller necessarily establishes the basis of conversation with the audience.

DA: That's breaking the fourth wall.

JL: Exactly. I think the storytelling art, as distinct from theater, is everyone being present, even as they allow themselves to be immersed in story. And this aspect of storytelling is a very good metaphor for critical presentation, as opposed to entertainment. Because if everyone is being only swept away by story, they will not remember the differentiation of material that a presenter is counting on their audience to leave the experience remembering. And finally, it's the obvious thing that the audience has the opportunity to change, either by being unresponsive or by injecting their own voice, ideas, requests into the process.

DA: That's true in theater and in storytelling. I can do the same show every night but it won't be the same experience. The best metaphor for my stories is that they are songs. Each of these story modules [songs] is well understood. The improvisation is the order in which I present each story segment and my lead-in to and exit from each story ... that's the jazz part. You have the little licks down that you understand, that are well-rehearsed, and then there is the way you reassemble them on a given evening. You respond to the audience. If you have an audience that is with you, that is responding—especially the ones that surprise you with a reaction to some improvised nugget that you were not expecting-you improve upon the work. I come up with some of my best material during the improvisational part of *Next Exit*. Just because something happens between me and that particular audience.

As I have performed the show more often, I've begun to get demands, like a popular singer, for special pieces, such as, "You have to do the *Dance of the Flaming Asshole*." Or I have had other surprises, as I recently had in a performance in the South Bay where I was doing my usual overview to the sixties, without telling any particular story, and somebody said, "Hey, who's that guy in the sweater?" The icon was an image of my college mentor, Ray Nash. So I told the story. I wasn't planning to, but somebody in my audience felt comfortable enough to ask and I felt that I could respond. There is something special about that.

There are other things you can do at the beginning of the show. For example, when my mother tells that story [recounting Dana's packing of a suitcase for a short trip as a young teenager] it absolutely defines my character. I think that's important. Who is this person that's telling a story up there? There are lots of ways to do this, but in my case there is nothing more definitive than that letter my mother wrote.

I also think that people relate to a story that defines where it all begins, like the story I tell of my grandmother [a tale about the beginning of the Atchley clan in this century]. I think a genesis story is important and is also relevant for businesses, because they have genesis stories to tell.

So you have the genesis story, the character story, and then you have the framework for the show. *Next Exit* can be done in a version with 12 stories in a half-hour or as an hour-and-a-half show. Every one of the stories that I tell in the early part of the show, from the1940s, has something down the road to pay off themes introduced from my youth. The notion of theme and variation, of being able to play out these strings of stories, is all part of a growing story bank.

JL: So there are multiple levels of story that can be set up and then pay off.

DA: Exactly. There can be multiple endings too. The most obvious one, the one I use the most, is the return to Newburyport, where I am turning with my dad and daughters. That story is the ultimate closer. [One of the stories introduced at the beginning of every show is a sequence of shots showing Dana's father and uncles as young men being marched in front of the camera in new suits and asked to turn in a circle. Baby Dana is introduced in the last sequence. He returns to the same spot 50 years later to perform the same turning sequence.]

JL: I think that you coast between the theater and storytelling metaphors, in that you have both a list of stories and an overarching story. Stage storytellers or musical storytellers do not feel that they have to have a throughline, although the best of them usually do create one.

DA: Right, it's like the Beatles' Sergeant Pepper concept album. Part of the challenge for me is how to create an interactive story experience with a middle, a beginning, and an end, but one that will never really be complete until I die. I think we figured it out. There is a completion. I think every show you feel gratified, even though at the end it says, "To Be Continued."

JL: You are not simply presenting data. The story arc has to have closure, it has to start well and end well, in order for it to really work.

DA: I think this is one of the extreme challenges for people who are trying to do interactive, working with multiple paths. If I were to put *Next Exit* on CD, I would appear and act as your guide, and you could wander at will, but have me return to offer suggestions and possible paths. The various attempts in creating interactive film and stories become labyrinthine narratives in which you lose that sense of closure. I think the ancient Greeks got it right. When you take away the traditional story arc, you might as well surf the Internet, because an endless labyrinth exploring people's stories and their links is going to be a much more intriguing interactive experience than the limited branching of a CD ROM story.

Corporate Consulting

JL: In your consultant practice, you are using storytelling in the context of professional presentations. How are you communicating the idea of storytelling to executives?

DA: Corporations generally hire multimedia production companies and agencies to create their brand-message stories. Many of these stories address the audience with a "voice of god" narrator that provides a high overview, integrated with fancy music and graphics. These presentations often don't resonate with the audience.

I have recently been working on a project with PricewaterhouseCoopers who sees digital storytelling as both a means to help top executives more effectively communicate as well as a way for all employees to communicate their brand message. In consulting with a vice president I suggested, "You are a storyteller. You are not a presenter." Recognizing this difference, he began to reframe his messages as stories.

JL: What kinds of stories?

DA: Well, I suggested these are the kinds of stories you tell people at dinner, at lunch, at business meetings, cocktails. You tell a lot of wonderful anecdotal stories all around what you are doing, why you are interested in it, and why you are involved. But those stories rarely are shared with your employees.

What we are trying to do with PricewaterhouseCoopers and with Coca-Cola, is to take a mixture of these well-produced little modules-which I call story segments-that can be produced in a somewhat more traditional manner, and intersperse those with these live segments where our presenters, our storytellers, ground them in their own point of view and their own personal stories. Every time you come out of one of these higher-level pieces you come right back to why this person is doing what he is doing and why she is standing there.

JL: Let's talk a little bit about your experiences with Coca-Cola. I mean how does Dana Atchley, digital storyteller, get hired by Coca-Cola?

DA: There was no way a couple of years ago that I could have gone and knocked on Coca-Cola's door and said, "I am a digital storyteller and you should be interested in this." They would have just said, "What are you talking about? Get out of here!" The fact is that somebody at Coca-Cola, who was in a position to make a decision, saw me perform. They saw it in a different venue, a museum [in Atlanta, as Dana was touring with *Next Exit*]. He later called me and said, "It was a choice between you and *Aida*, and I decided to see as much of your show as possible and then go see *Aida*. I saw something there, the possibility that what you were doing could be helpful for working with one of our top executives."

I was asked to help the president of Coca-Cola become more of a storyteller or, as I perceived it, less "buttoned up." Some CEOs are good storytellers, and the CEO is generally considered to be the "guardian of the brand," the spokesperson. Some speak well and some are terrified. Mr. Ivester [then president, now CEO of Coca-Cola] had been a chief financial officer. Now he was in a position where he was having to deal with the brand story and he was presenting material that people were writing for him—"Ok, here's your script"—with somebody else putting together the presentational elements, a PowerPoint presentation. All of a sudden, the person from Coca-Cola's (who had seen *Next Exit*) light bulb went on: "Mr. Ivester's got some interesting personal stories, and if he could combine those with brand stories, this could work. And if he could see what you were doing, he would get it." And he did.

The story I tell about this experience is a good one. Three years ago, there was no way I could have conceived of doing what I am doing now. You do what you believe in, what your heart tells you, and all of a sudden opportunity opens up. Mr. Ivester didn't really react to my show. There were 14 people in a room, and he was eight feet in front of me, and he just sat there. He might have smiled once or twice but not enough to get anything back. And, of course, how were the other people reacting? They were reacting the way he was reacting. After the show he did not come up and say, "That was interesting"—which is always scary—or "I like that" or just leave. He says, "What does Coca-Cola mean to you?"

That was his first comment to me. It was like a hold-up, I mean, I really felt like he stuck a gun at me, and that if I didn't answer right, I was going to get a bullet in the gut. And I told a couple of stories. And I know the person who brought me down there is thinking, "Oh f---, do I still have a job?" And then Mr. Ivester said, "You know that story you told about the little girl in the second grade? [Dana's first experience with romantic pining.] Well I've got one like that, only I married her." I knew I had connected, and he left the room. My contact came back and said, "Well Mr. Ivester thinks you have had a troubled life but said, 'Let's do something with this guy.'"

As I look back on it and tell this story over and over again in corporate or presentation environments, the thing that strikes me most about the story was that question, "What does Coca-Cola mean to you?" Because that is the key question in a corporation that you need to know as the CEO, as an employee, as a marketing person, as an assistant. You need to understand how consumers will answer that question. Because if you take the sum total of those responses about what Coca-Cola-or substitute any other brand-means to you, you will begin to understand what the brand means. The power of that brand, not as it's been defined by the agencies and marketing group, but as it is really defined, by what it means to people. And how you find out is by asking that question, of yourself and other people. It was a hold-up, but it was a hell of a good question. So I work with that all the time. I think you can also ask that question on a personal basis. We ask people in the digital storytelling workshop, "Why are you telling this story?" If we answer that question, and answer it honestly, we'll get to a core value of what we are doing, and it will certainly help to define what we are doing.

JL: You could also build these brand stories by asking the consumer what the brand means to them.

DA: Of course, that is what we did with Coca-Cola at the World of Coca-Cola in Las Vegas. As a service company, PricewaterhouseCoopers doesn't have those kinds of consumers, so where they get their stories is going to be different.

They define their brand as "Peoples, Worlds, and Knowledge." Well "worlds" is a kind of slippery one and "knowledge" I am beginning to get a handle on through people like Bob Johansen [of the Institute for the Future] and Lin Knapp [chief information officer for PricewaterhouseCoopers]. "Peoples" was a much more intriguing one. I don't know if I showed you this gorgeous book by a company called Interbrand out of Amsterdam. They really got the people issue. You look at these images and stories, and you say, "Wow, look at these people. These are amazing people." And then you look and notice they also happen to be somebody's personal assistant or a director of this or that at PricewaterhouseCoopers.

JL: I think the important point is that the concept of brand cannot always develop from the top down. People, either as employees or consumers, may invest in brand identity values that you never intended, and allowing their stories to trickle up to the top is what expands and truly defines the brand.

DA: But you have to encourage people to be storytellers, starting with the executives, and then spreading out across the company, because then people will get permission to be storytellers. Part of what *Next Exit* offers, as a larger idea, and I am absolutely clear on this, is what Apple Computer used to call the "excellent design example." People go, "Oh, I get it, I can see what digital technology can do." Secondly, it gives people permission to tell their own story. Those are two very important things: an excellent example and permission.

That is, in fact, what people like Mr. Dauphinais at PricewaterhouseCoopers have to do: give an excellent design example, and then without saying so overtly, give people the sense that they have a story as well. Make them think, "I have good one, and maybe you would like to hear it." Well, obviously, if you have 2,000 people at the meeting you can't hear every one, but if you use the Intranet you can do that.

JL: Do you have any speculation about the future direction of this work?

DA: Well, I have never been much of a speculator, I am much more of a doer. That's why it just boggles the mind that I am working with organizations like the Institute for the Future that spends so much of their time speculating and trying to plan the future. I figure the future grows from the present. In deciding in 1988 to begin working on *Next Exit*, everything I have done since has grown from that action. Otherwise I would still be shooting computer-training tapes.

The past seven years we have seen some incredible advances: relatively cheap computers and software and a new medium of distribution. I think the computer as a device for storytelling, coupled with easier software for telling your stories and the Internet as a disintermediated distribution device, are everything we could have dreamed.

Appendix A

The World of Digital Storytellling

While this book has emphasized our the methods of training and approach developed by the Center for Digital Storytelling, practitioners of Digital Storytelling could include anyone concerned with producing creative work on a computer who has a high appreciation of the narrative arts (poetry, storytelling, theater, fiction, essays, film) informing their design. Below we discuss some of the possibilities and representative examples.

The Digital Storyteller in Performance

Theater and the performing arts in the 20th century have integrated every available communication technology—from the use of recordings to state-of-the-art multimedia-while traditional storytellers have generally remained at the low-tech end of the innovation spectrum.

Perhaps as a result, Dana Atchley's *Next Exit* was a singular example of the integration of interactive media and the traditional performance storyteller. We are aware of a few other efforts—notably the work of rock musicians Todd Rundgren and Graham Nash—to create one-man shows.

Beyond the context of traditional storytelling, there have been many artists and organizations that have explored digital applications in theater. Many artists have developed their work side-by-side with the engineers and technologists creating the newest tools of the Information Age. New York's Laurie Anderson and San Francisco's George Coates Performance Works have pioneered addressing the impact of the Internet, distributed computing, and virtual reality. We have also seen a steady stream of work in new media and performance emerge from NYU, MIT Media Lab, Arizona State and the University of Texas at Austin.

Hypertext

Since the early sixties, the goal of one segment of the information technology research community was to create a hypertextual environment to assist in the tasks of citation and referencing—an essential part of academic activity. The World Wide Web developed many of its principal features from the design lessons developed by the hypertext community.

At the same time, a number of academics interested in the potential literary applications of hypertext began collaborating on creating content. Since the mid-eighties a number of hypertext novels, essays, and short stories were created, exploring a broad range of content. The hypertext movement also developed a series of tools and aesthetic principles to inform their work.

Our community of digital storytellers has only recently begun a more active dialogue with the hypertext community. Eastgate Systems in Boston has remained the center of both publication and dialogue about the hypertext community, and a visit to their Web site (www.eastgate.com) is a great way to learn about titles and the issues in the hypertext community.

Interactive Digital Storytelling

The advent of laserdisc and CD-ROM technologies ushered in the era of interactive storytelling through rich multiple media. CD-ROMs have been associated primarily with the computer game market. While games undoubtedly have narrative attributes, we have only met a small number of game developers who view the narrative concerns of their work as more than trivial. The success of *Myst* demonstrated that significant attention to story could make a huge difference in how an audience responds to the "puzzle" aspects of the game.

A large number of academic and noncommercial artistic efforts have created CD-ROMs and are beginning to create DVDs with specific narrative concerns. Historically, we look back at Abbe Don's *We Make Memories*, an extraordinarily rich exploration of four generations of women in her family, as one of the first design examples of storytelling and interactivity. Created in 1992, Pedro Meyer's *I Photograph to Remember*, which documents Pedro's parents' final struggle with cancer, remains one of the most emotionally compelling stories of this form. We also count as colleagues Greg Roach and Jon Sanborn, who have developed a number of commercial titles that explore interactive video. Greg's *Quantum Gate* titles and the development of the notion of virtual film as demonstrated in his 1998 *X-Files* CD-ROM by his company, Hyperbole, and Sanborn's *Psychic Detective* CD-ROM were part of our dialogue. And our community was equally moved and impressed by *I Am a Singer* by Australian multimedia designer Megan Heyward, *Mauve Desert* by Adrienne Jenek, and, *Ceremony of Innocence* (an adaptation of Nick Bantock's *Griffin and Sabine* trilogy) by Alex Mayhew.

In all of these interactive narratives, like their hypertext equivalents, navigational design is a critical part of their aesthetic success or failure. The more artistically successful have a consistent navigational mechanism for the users to stay in touch with the story arc—such as the ability to see the story as a linear event from beginning to end. They also tend to create a dialogue with the user that deepens or extends the user's emotional connection to the story line—either by calling for their direct participation as characters that can shape the story's resolution, or in inquiring about the users response to material that is presented.

Web-Based Storytelling

The Web has mirrored the hypertext and CD-ROM multimedia authoring worlds with a myriad of different narrative experiments. There are purely hypertextual works, works that use text and a minimum of images, and increasingly media-rich work that approaches what has been done in the fixed media arena. Many of us point to Joseph Squier's *Life With Father* as an early, but inspiring example of a moving and effective Web story.

Three phenomena have dominated the storytelling uses of the Web. The first was the Web serial, essentially a soap opera format Web site, with daily or weekly updates. In the mid-nineties, Yahoo! listed about 120 Web serials, now there are nine. The first major serial of this genre was *The Spot*, a look behind the lives of some youthful Southern Californians, aimed at the "Bay Watch" or "Melrose Place" fan. There are ways for the audience to interact with the story line, or in the case of *The Spot*, with the characters. We worked with artist Jon Sanborn to create his *Paul Is Dead* Web serial in 1997, a complex mystery that invites the users to uncover the truth behind the death of a rock star. The interactive television market is still a gleam in the eyes of many, but we may be years before this takes hold as a genre in itself.

The other storytelling phenomenon that emerged early on in the Web's development is the Web diary. Justin Hall's *Links.net* is one of the better known examples. He has traveled the country and world documenting his life for an audience of at times thousands. Hundreds, if not thousands, of diaries exist. Many of the sites blur the boundaries between thoughtful literature and exhibitionism, fiction and nonfiction.

Finally, there is the phenomena of the storytelling exchanges in the context of writing communities. Part of the Internet's allure is the fluid sense of private and public it creates. The posting of intimate aspects of life stories invites intense, and often dramatic, interchanges between authors and their audience. Sites like Derek Powazek's *the fray* (fray.com) approach this with artful intentions, curating personal essays on many sensitive topics that directly invite readers to respond with personal stories of their own. This type of storytelling interaction encourages community, connecting diverse people through shared experience.

Multiplayer Role-Playing Games— From MUDS to Virtual Reality

Many people have explored the narrative potential of online role playing in the mid-nineties. Role-playing environments encompass everything from the text-based multiuser dungeon (MUD) and the object-oriented MUD (MOO) to online virtual worlds using character avatars like The Palace, to more sophisticated explorations of virtual reality where three-dimensional controls are linked directly to the player's physical movements through VR helmets and gloves.

While these forms have evolved to online gaming environments, all of these forms invite a level of conversational exchange, which can include sharing stories in-character. Playing the games inherently requires a strong sense of narrative intelligence, how to portray and sustain a character, how to develop a situation to a crisis and resolution, etc. The dramatic success of a given experience-or a long-term relationship to the game-relies on the improvisational skill of the players, the situations in which they find themselves, and the robustness of the virtual environment's interactivity. At the current state of technology and user sophistication, many of these environments remain at level of awkward social interaction—chat with pictures—that does not encourage prolonged or serious participation.

The designers of online games are increasingly aware of how story structure enables them to heighten dramatic tension. All of the more successful environments involve a metastory—a larger goal or activity in which the participants are simultaneously involved, from community building to defeating an opposing force.

Janet Murray of MIT has suggested in her book, *Hamlet on the Holodeck*, that the authoring of these virtual worlds leads us precisely to the territory of the new aesthetic development of cyberdrama. While no specific environment that meets all of her requirements for cyberdramatics currently exists, she outlines the elements necessary to successfully implement an authored world. These include conventions for interaction and rituals of participation; a complex and media-rich world that sustains a constant injection of plot material; and sophisticated computer-generated characterizations that make the players' interactions continuously unpredictable and spontaneous.

Appendix B

Caveat Emptor— Creating a Digital Storytelling Production Environment

When asked almost every other day about the shopping list for establishing either a computer lab or personal workstation for producing digital stories, my answer for ten years has been the same question, "How much money do you have?"

What is clear is that we have crossed the border of relatively affordable (sub $1000 US) solutions, from Apple's iMac and iMovie software and a digital camera to a low cost PC with a number of hardware/software packages that could get you started.

I was told in the early part of the twentieth century there were 2000 car companies in North America, and I assume, like the 1990's technology industries, they debated design, as in, where to put the clutch, brake and gas pedal. Digital Media tools are still in an evolutionary state where some of the basics are not completely resolved. As such, there are no guarantees that what you have, or what you buy, will actually work in a consistent manner.

Our approach to survival in the floating crap game of the computer and media industries is by no means systematic. CDS is a small, underfunded non-profit, which puts us in league with about 80% of the consumers and 50% of the professional users of these sets of tools. Like most of you, we have made choices by necessity, choices by trial and error, and once in awhile choices based on research and polling our peers in the larger community.

As a buying guide for your home, school, work or lab, we want to outline the issues and approaches we take to the present digital media environment. Drop by the web site in six months, and see what we have updated.

In our communications with colleagues hosting the workshop in a computer lab, we recommend the following basic list of hardware.

- One computer workstation for each project.

- A Teacher's workstation connected to media projector with speakers, for tutorials.

- One scanner for every six participants

- A video capture station (if the computers are not video capable) with a dedicated computer able to digitize from VHS and Hi8.

- Hi8 camera or DV camera for the video capture station with appropriate cables

- VCR

- An audio set up in a separate room from the lab for audio recording. Ideally we have a computer with a mixing board, microphone on a stand

- Printer networked to student's stations

- The appropriate software to operate the tasks in media production, scanning, audio capture, video and audio editing, word processing, printing, and networking.

Let's review each of these components.

Workstations

1999 represents the coming of the G3 Apple microprocessor and in 2000 the Intel Pentium 3 microprocessor which along with improved Video RAM and acceleration boosted the capacity for computers to handle video playback at relatively consistent levels. Random Access Memory became relatively inexpensive, and computers began to ship with 256 MB which was a reasonable minimum for high quality video. Finally, hard drives became large and cheap enough to satisfy the voracious appetite for video, almost 210 MB per minute at the highest resolution. Video remains one of the most demanding applications for a computer, so generally, if it can handle the minimum requirements of the side of your video editing software application, it can handle about any other software you are going to throw at it in the digital story production process.

Of course you need a monitor, a keyboard and a mouse. Big monitors do help with video production but do not let someone sell you one as a requirement.

Cameras

If you have been using a 35mm film camera and scanning images, and then switch to a digital camera at a price point below $500, it would not surprise us if you went back to film. But Digital Cameras are improving daily, and they provide numerous arguments for their ease of use and economy in a multimedia environment. If you have the money now, or can wait another two years, the inexpensive digital camera really will be compatible in quality with film cameras of a similar price. As for brands, we have liked our Nikon Coolpix, but the Olympus, Canon, and Minolta cameras all seem comparable.

Digital Video

This is another competitive world where consumers benefit from the nature of the current marketplace. DV has three real levels of cost/quality in the current market, sub $1000, $1000-$2000, and above $2000. The average sub $1000 or consumer level camera is extraordinary for the price, and will service almost any family, school or home use. In the middle, more feature sets, more compactness, slightly better quality. Above $2000, you begin to have much better quality because of 3 Chips that process the color, as well as features like balanced audio. Feature Films are being shot with $4000 Canon XL-1 cameras, so I can not think why anyone would spend more than this on a camera who is not fully in the film business. The brands, Sony, Canon, Panasonic.

Video Capture

In 1999, Apple Computer introduced the Firewire/IEEE 1394 input connection which has provided a standardized mechanism for linking cameras and computers. PC makers are only now in 2002 making this input standard in their computers. Standardization means you can more or less take any Digital Video camera and connect it to a computer and start capturing the video, and outputting it back to your camera or tape deck to view on your television. More or less suggests that particularly with PCs, everything has to be working correctly, and if the machines were not configured for video capture (the Sony VAIO computers for example make this standard) it may not work without the typical PC trial and error, calling tech support or getting uncle Vinnie, or some teenager to come fix it for you. Most Video Editing software have capture mechanisms for video.

Audio Capture

Surprisingly, this is no easy feat still on many computers, including some Apple computers (like one generation of the G4 Laptops and some G4 towers). On PC, the built in Sound Recorder software is a throw back to the relative Pleistocene era of Windows. We suggest a software like Syntrillium Software 's CoolEdit to assist you with capturing audio on a PC. On a Mac, you can use most Video Editing software and the native Quicktime capabilities to assist you with audio capture.

We recommend you getting a professional microphone (a rugged Shure 58 or a good condenser mic if you don't have kids that will scream in it all day), Mic Stand, and small Mixer (Behringer or Mackie's cheapest choice). This assists you working with voice ranges from loud to soft, and no software is going to solve a bad capture of audio.

Scanning/Image Production

Perfectly good scanners have gotten so cheap they give them away with computers now, but you still want a copy of a tool like Photoshop Elements or full Photoshop to assist you and your scanner with image manipulation and production. We also have used a reasonably good digital camera, a tripod and a couple of lamps (or a nice spot outside) to set up a photo stand to quickly photograph images and books. This process saves on the scanning time and often creates usable images for multimedia and video.

Video Software

Here is where the grass is greener on the Mac with both iMovie built in, and the availability of a complicated workhorse like Final Cut Pro. On the PC side, Pinnacle Systems has Studio 7, the best iMovie equivalent, and a host of other DV and Analog capture and editing systems. We use Adobe Premiere because it represents a mid-range product that still can be taught to beginners, or at least we can teach it, we don't suggest you start with this in the classroom or home. Premiere also works on Apple's as well as PC machines.

Other Software

We live and die by two post-production softwares, Discreet's Cleaner 6 and Roxio's Toast Titanium. The first, Cleaner, is what compresses batches of movies to prepare them for CD ROM, DVD, Web or other uses. The second helps to burn the hundreds of CD's we use to store material. As DVDs get cheaper we will move to DVD for both storage and presentation, stay tuned for the software options.

Of course word processing and Web applications should be thought of in the lab for scripting and research.

Networks

We have found having a robust and "user" friendly network eases the process. Let me repeat the "user-friendly" part for all the network Nazis running school and business networks like high security prisons. Multimedia production requires a great deal of adaptable network movement of files and material. If accessing the network is too complicated for the participants the entire process collapses. Multimedia production, especially video, is not suited to being done from a server across a network, so having a good system for storing the elements during production on the production workstation, and backing up the material on servers after all production is complete is a must.

Spending Money

Another thing we have found from long experience is to never by the latest coolest thing when it releases, whether software or hardware. They always get it wrong at first, and then fix it for about six months. While it true the next newest coolest thing comes out every six months, ignore the hype, your machine has a reasonable shelf life of two to five years. We look forward to re-cycled computing, where the shell and most of the hardware remains the same, and the guts get changed to keep up with Moore's Law and other innovations. Computer waste is an enormous, enormous environmental hazard.

The Computing Appliance—A Final Editorial Note

In chapter two, the argument was made that we are moving toward the memory box, a computing appliance that makes storing the artifacts of your life experience, and giving you the power to creatively transform them into powerful stories, as accessible as your VCR. Besides the fact that most of us can not program our VCRs to begin with, we should also be frank that the computing industry does not seem that interested in appliances, machines made as a number of elegant and easy to use components, any more than they seem interested in re-cyclable computers.

The industry has been trapped in an economic nightmare of stock option greed and cut throat competition that makes elegance the last thing on any one's mind. Computer marketing was built on the notion of "power" and "features," and healthy dose of built in obsolescence. What if a computer manufacturer took the tact of the old Maytag advertisement about the bored maintenance technicians never having to work because a Maytag washer never broke? Can we imagine a multimedia computing appliance that would do what we need it to do for 20 years?!

The current recession may cause enough damage in these industries to have some enterprising entrepreneurs realize that normal people are exhausted by computer hype, and endless, usually pointless, innovations and upgrades. It may not make more billionaires out of the CEO's of these companies, but it will make a market, and the memory box will likely emerge.

Appendix C
Web Resources for Digital Storytelling

The Center for Digital Storytelling maintains an ongoing list of Web resources about digital storytelling and storytelling activities. The list can be found online at www.storycenter.org/links.html.

Principal Resource Sites

Center for Digital Storytelling; www.storycenter.org

> The online home for our center in Berkeley, California.

Digital Storytelling Association: www.dsaweb.org

> The home website of the international organization of Digital Storytelling.

Hillary McLellan's Story Link: http://tech-head.com/dstory.htm

> Researcher/Educator/Digital Storyteller Hillary McLellan's site has the most complete link section.

Digital Storytelling Festival: www.dstory.com

> The home website of the annual digital storytelling event in Crested Butte, Colorado 1995-1999.

Dana Atchley's Next Exit: www.nextexit.com

> Home of Dana's archive and background on his work in professional and artistic contexts.

Eastgate Systems: www.eastgate.com

> Eastgate is the home of the hypertext and acts as educational resource, a hub of theory and practice, and store for the electronic literary community.

CDS Case Study Programs

Capture Wales: www.bbc.co.uk/wales/capturewales

> The BBC in Wales/Cymru has developed an ongoing program in digital storytelling gathering stories from people throughout the country.

Digital Clubhouse Network: www.digiclub.org

> CDS was instrumental in the establishment and development of the Digital Storytelling Programs at the two Digital Clubhouses in Sunnyvale, CA and New York City.

Managing Information in Rural America: http://mira.wkkf.org

> Supported by the W.K.K. Kellogg Foundation, MIRA was a multi-year program assisting grassroots community activists and organizations in developing technology assessments and development plans. CDS helped them to tell the stories of the process.

War and Remembrance: http://209.197.234.10/kcs/index.html

> Working with the Kansas City Symphony and the Learning Exchange, a Kansas City based curriculum design company, CDS assisted in developing a program for the local schools for a concert dedicated to the issues of war and peace.

Future Visions: www.waittfoundation.org/event4.html

> In conjunction with the Institute for the Future and the Waitt Family Foundation, CDS helped a group of eastside San Diego residents share stories about their feeling and thoughts on the role of technology in their community in the future.

D*LAB: www.storyvault.org

> From 1995-1998, CDS organized a youth program, under the direction of Ron Light, that helped to work with students and create stories with San Francisco youth.

Design Examples and Communities

Bubbe's Back Porch: www.bubbe.com

Abbe Don's interactive storytelling site that includes stories and processes from Digital Story Bee, a women's story circle.

John Freyer: www.allmylifeforsale.com and www.temporama.com

John decided to sell every last item of his belongings besides his car, laptop and digital camera on Ebay, and then meet and document his buyers and the final resting places of his things.

The Fray: www.fray.com and www.fray.org

Perhaps the best ongoing example of how story and community intermingle, Derek Powazek has built a large network of contributors and audiences exploring the use of shared, well written personal narratives as the basis for connecting people together. Derek is also connected to a "ring" of excellent designers and writers including:

Maggie Donea	www.kia.net/maggy,
Lance Arthur	www.glassdog.com,
Heather Champ	www.harrumph.com,
Magdalena Powers	www.foolsparadise.org, and
Miles Hochstein	http://documentedlife.com

among dozens of others.

Justin Hall: www.links.net

Perhaps Jack Kerouac re-incarnated with a web journal. Justin's words and worlds defy categorization, but along with a hundred thousand or so other web journals, blogs, and web-based diaries, he suggests a core notion of story for the digital age.

Alex Rivera: www.alexrivera.com

Alex's Invisible America and Cybracero mockumentary is both pointed and humorous, like many web activists, he is looking at how connect social satire with political action.

Third World Majority: http://cultureisaweapon.org

TWM is a collective of young women of color working in media training and production resource center dedicated to global justice

Silence Speaks: www.silencespeaks.org

As a project of the Third World Majority organization, the site presents Digital Storytelling in Support of Healing and Violence Prevention.

Creative Narrations: www.creativenarrations.net

Community-based storytelling resource in Somerville, Massachusetts

The Mom Project: www.uiowa.edu/~arted/epaulos

Emily Paulos explores art, technology, and storytelling in this family history site.

The Photobus: www.photobus.co.uk

Daniel Meadows' site revolves around a simple but provocative idea, what you returned to photograph a selection of people from towns across England 25 years later, in the same pose and context.

Zone Zero: www.zonezero.com

Pedro Meyer has created a quintessential photography site featuring fascinating work from around the world. As part of the exhibitions, he asked all the participating artists to share their thoughts, and often links the exhibitions to narratives.

Design Issues

Nathan Shedroff: www.nathan.com

One of the leading creatives looking at issues of experience and interaction design

Lynda Weinman; www.lynda.com

Queen of the web color palette, and also a leading proponent of new media authoring in Flash and other web tools

International Centers for Digital Storytelling

Capture Wales (Wales, UK): www.bbc.co.uk/wales/capturewales

Evision (Wellington, New Zealand): www.evision.co.nz

Australian Center for the Moving Image: www.acmi.net.au

MediaLinx Habitat at the Canadian Film Centre: www.cdnfilmcentre.com

Digital Bridge (Sweden): www.digitalbridge.nu/sidor/db.html

Proseed (Tokyo, Japan): www.proseed.co.jp

Educational Examples

Idida Movie: www.alaskacenter.org/idida_movie/index.html

Scott County, KY: www.scott.k12.ky.us/technology/digitalstorytelling/ds.html

Lexington, MA: www.infotoday.com/MMSchools/jan02/banaszewski.htm

Bibliography

Digital Storytelling

Johnson, Steven. *Interface Culture*. San Francisco: HarperSanFrancisco, 1997.

Joyce, Michael. *Of Two Minds: Hypertext Pedagogy and Poetics*. Ann Arbor, University of Michigan Press, 1996.

Laurel, Brenda. *Computers As Theatre*. Menlo Park: Addison-Wesley, 1993.

Murray, Janet H. *Hamlet on the Holodeck: The Future of Narrative in Cyberspace*. New York: The Free Press, 1997.

Sloane, Sarah. *Digital Fictions: Storytelling in a Material World*. New York, Ablex Corp., 2000.

Turkle, Sherry. *Life on the Screen: Identity in the Age of the Internet*. New York: Touchstone, 1997.

Ilana Snyder. *Page to Screen*. London, Routledge, 1998.

General Storytelling and/or Public Speaking

Birch, Carol L., and Melissa A. Heckler, eds. *Who Says?* Little Rock, AR: August House Publishers, 1996.

Cassady, Marsh. *The Art of Storytelling: Creative Ideas for Preparation and Performance*. Colorado Springs: Meriwether Publishing, 1994.

Davis, Donald. *Telling Your Own Stories*. Little Rock, AR: August House Publishers, 1993.

Mooney, Bill, and David Holt. *The Storyteller's Guide*. Little Rock, AR: August House Publishers, 1996.

Robbins, Jo. *High Impact Presentations: A Multimedia Approach*. New York: John Wiley and Sons, 1997.

Creative Writing and/or Autobiography

Case, Patricia Ann. *How to Write Your Autobiography*. Santa Barbara, CA: Woodbridge Press, 1995.

Egri, Lajos. *The Art of Dramatic Writing*. New York: Simon and Schuster, 1946.

Goldberg, Natalie. *Writing Down the Bones*. Boston: Sambala, 1986.

Lamott, Anne. *Bird by Bird*. New York: Pantheon Books, 1994.

Maquire, Jack. *The Power of Personal Storytelling*. New York, Tarcher-Putnum. 1998.

Metzger, Deena. *Writing for Your Life*. San Francisco: Harper Collins, 1992.

Polking, Kirk. *Writing Family Histories and Memoirs*. Cincinnati, OH: Betterway Books, 1995.

Rainer, Tristine. *Your Life As Story*. New York: G.P. Putnam's Sons, 1997.

Selling, Bernard. *Writing From Within*. Alameda, CA: Hunter House, 1988.

Stone, Richard. *The Healing Art of Storytelling*. New York, Hyperion, 1996.

Ueland, Brenda. *If You Want to Write*. Saint Paul, MN: Graywolf Press, 1938.

Design and Applications

Bone, Jan, and Ron Johnson. *Understanding the Film: An Introduction to Film Appreciation*. NTC, 1996.

Horn, Robert. *Visual Language*. Macro VQ Press, 1999.

Laurel, Brenda. *Utopian Entrepreneur*. Cambridge. MIT Press, 2001.

McCloud, Scott. *Understanding Comics*. New York: Kitchen Sink Press, 1993.

McCloud, Scott. *Reinventing Comics*. New York: Perennial, 2000.

McKee, Robert. *Story; Substance, Structure, Style and the Principles of Screenwriting*. Regan Books/Harper Collins, 1997

Powazek, Derek. *Design for Community*. Indianapolis, New Riders, 2002.

Shedroff, Nathan. *Experience Design 1*. Indianapolis, New Riders, 2001.

Storytelling and Education

Bruner, Jerome. *The Culture of Education*. Cambridge, MA: Harvard University Press, 1996.

Egan, Kieran. *Teaching As Story Telling*. Chicago: The University of Chicago Press, 1986.

Egan, Kieran. *The Educated Mind: How Cognitive Tools Shape our Understanding*. Chicago: The University of Chicago Press, 1997.

Gillis, Candida. *The Community As Classroom*. Portsmouth, NH: Boynton/ Cook, 1992.

Winston, Linda. *Keepsakes: Using Family Stories in Elementary Classrooms*. Portsmouth, NH: Heinemann, 1997.

Cognitive Theory, Psychology, and Narrative

Dennett, Daniel. *Kinds of Minds: Toward an Understanding of Consciousness.* New York: Basic Books, 1996.

Gardner, Howard. *Frames of Mind.* New York: Basic Books, 1993.

Harvey, John H. *Embracing Their Memory: Loss and the Social Psychology of Storytelling.* Needham Heights, MA: Allyn and Bacon, 1996.

Hunt, Celia. *Therapeutic Dimensions of Autobiography in Creative Writing.* London, Jessica Kingsley Publishers, 2000.

Kast, Verena. *Folktales as Therapy.* New York: Fromm International, 1995.

Kurtz, Ernest. *The Spirituality of Imperfection.* New York. Bantam, 1992.

Linde, Charlotte. *Life Stories: The Creation of Coherence.* Oxford: Oxford University Press, 1993.

McAdams, Dan P. *The Stories We Live By,* New York, Guilford Press, 1993

Ong, Walter J. *Orality and Literacy: The Technologizing of the Word.* London: Routledge, 1982.

Parry, Alan and Robert E. Doan. *Story Re-Visions: Narrative Therapy in the Postmodern World.* New York: The Guilford Press, 1994.

Schank, Roger C. *Tell Me a Story: Narrative and Intelligence.* Evanston, IL: Northwestern University Press, 1990.

Corporate Contexts

Denning, Stephen. *The Springboard*. Boston. BH, 2001.

Fetterman, Roger. *The Interactive Corporation*. New York: Random House, 1997.

Senge, Peter M. *The Fifth Discipline: The Art & Practice of the Learning Organization*. New York: Doubleday, 1994.

Ware, James P., et al. *The Search of Digital Excellence*. New York: McGraw-Hill, 1997.

General

Birkerts, Sven. *The Gutenberg Elegies*. New York: Ballantine, 1994.

Campbell, Joseph. *The Power of Myth*. New York: Doubleday, 1988.

Gilster, Paul. *Digital Literacy*. New York: John Wiley and Sons, Inc., 1997.

Goleman, Daniel. *Emotional Intelligence*. New York: Bantam Books, 1995.

McLuhan, Marshall. *Understanding Media: The Extensions of Man*. Cambridge, MA: The MIT Press, 1994.

Index

The cover of this book was designed and produced in Adobe Photoshop 6.0, using the Stone Sans and Palatino fonts. The Memory Box illustration was drawn by Jos Sances at Alliance Graphics. The collage was created by Joe Lambert and Emily Paulos at the Center for Digital Storytelling. The photograph on the back cover was shot by Emily Paulos.

The interior of this book is set in Adobe's Stone Sans and Stone Serif fonts, and was produced in FrameMaker 5.5.6.